Obamistan!
Land Without Racism

Your Guide to the New America

damali ayo

Lawrence Hill Books

Library of Congress Cataloging-in-Publication Data
ayo, damali.
  Obamistan! land without racism : your guide to the new America / damali ayo.
    p. cm.
  ISBN 978-1-56976-243-1 (pbk.)
  1. United States—Race relations—Humor. 2. African Americans—Social conditions—21st century—Humor. 3. Travel—Guidebooks—Humor. 4. Satire. I.
Title.
  PN6231.R25A96 2010
  818'.607—dc22

                                                            2009046561

Cover design: Sarah Olson
Cover photographs: istockphoto/Michael Krinke (Asian woman); istockphoto/
Photo Euphoria (African-American man); istockphoto/arsenik (Caucasian
woman); istockphoto/Salih Guler (dog and cat)
Interior design: Sarah Olson
Interior images: damali ayo

© 2010 by damali ayo
All rights reserved
Published by Lawrence Hill Books
An Imprint of Chicago Review Press, Incorporated
814 North Franklin Street
Chicago, Illinois 60610
ISBN 978-1-56976-243-1
Printed in the United States of America
5 4 3 2 1

Acknowledgments

Thank you to Annin Barrett, Heather Day, Rosie Finn, Charmelle Green, Marc Gerald, Anu Gupta, Christos Ikonomopoulos, Stevie Madison, Elisabeth Malzahn, Dwayne McDuffie, Barbara and Bill Patterson, Kim Patterson, Kana Suppaiah, Richard Tarlaian, Yuval Taylor, Sandy Tolan, and Patricia Williams.

A very special thank-you to the always amiable Eric Okorie. Jai ma.

This is for the fourth black president.

Contents

E

F

G

H

I

J

L

M

• • •

Post Obamistan 185

Appendix 187

Introduction

A Dream Fulfilled

For centuries Americans waged a war of wills against themselves. An epic love-hate race war was played out in every corner of American society, from Barbies to barrios, from four square to foreclosures. Then, shockingly, on November 4, 2008, with the swift strikes of swarms of synchronized voters, Americans gave prejudice and discrimination a boot to the behind just the way the founding fathers did with ol' King George at the dawn of the nation. In this new land, the pride of this accomplishment echoed from mountaintops to bus stops, from mini-mansions to tenement houses, as Americans streaked through the streets with tears streaming down their faces, crying, "Racism is over!"

True to the pioneering spirit that started this country, and emboldened by millions of brave voices chanting choruses of

"Change!" on that historic day, you, the citizens of the United States, made a radical leap unparalleled by any nation in the history of the world. You took a dark horse of a candidate and made him your main stud. You and your fellow patriots transformed a person who on any given day in Old America would have been racially profiled by the police, framed for carrying a concealed weapon, brutally prosecuted, falsely convicted, wrongfully imprisoned, and very likely given the death penalty, into your commander in chief and put his finger on the trigger of the largest cache of nuclear weapons and gun-wielding soldiers on the planet. You gave this man, whom in prior times you feared would jack your car keys, the keys to the highest office in the land. A man who, merely months earlier, could have only found success as a basketball player or rap star became the leader of the free world. This earth-shattering move signaled not only the end of racism but restored America's righteous place as the ballsiest country on earth.

Ending racism is a feat of majestic proportions, dwarfing the building of the pyramids, surpassing the fall of the Berlin Wall, and eclipsing the elusive "peace in the Middle East." Like its most treasured superhero, America stepped into Superman's phone booth as an awkward, closed-minded country, consigned to a meager, plodding life. Then, in a flash, the phone booth door swung open and a dashing new America jumped out—unfettered, enlightened, and recharged—with its vast multi-colored cape waving in the wind as it launched to the sky to relay its message of progress and hope to the world. America was reinvented—soaring through the clouds, looking down at its ant-sized past.

What does this dramatic evolution mean for you? Well, you might not always recognize parts of your country. You might be surprised at how many things changed with the fall of racism. You might feel as if you are a visitor in this new land. This guide will help you familiarize yourself with this new, exciting adventure of a country. It's almost like traveling abroad without ever leaving home.

Of course, the first and most obvious change is what you call this place and those in it. Clever New Americans, hungry to leave the past behind, chose a fresh new name for this bright new country. In honor of the chosen vessel of change, this magical place is called "Obamistan." You will find that your fellow New Americans playfully refer to each other as "Obamistanis," signaling a tattoo-like commitment to the humble yet stalwart servant you voted into office. Obamistanis show off their new nationality with pride. Some outsiders, confused by the sound of the word, have placed Obamistanis on their list of Islamic terrorists. But the fearless resilience of the Obamistani spirit shines forth. When criticized for "sounding Muslim," Obamistanis respond, "Well, my middle name is Hussein!"

Pinch Yourself. Yep, You're Awake.

Hooray! Some of you are probably starting every day with a big pat on the back for all the work you did to make this moment happen, and you cannot wait to see what's changed. You canvassed and donated to the Obama campaign; you may have even made a few friends of other races along the way. You haven't stayed in contact with them since, but that doesn't matter. If you did not work on the campaign, you surely voted for Obama or at the very least you got drunk at the party when he won the big prize, right? Right. You basically invented Obamistan.

Maybe your experience has been different. Maybe you are excited that your country finally elected a black president so now all the clamoring and moaning about diversity and affirmative action can end. You'll be happy when all the racial bean counting is over and people go back to being people again. Maybe you feel that the fall of racism was simply the natural order of things—no big deal. America was virtually over racism before it elected a black guy anyhow. What could you have to learn? You went to school with a few black kids, didn't everyone?

Or maybe you didn't work very hard to make this moment happen. Maybe you even voted for the other guy. That's OK. Obamistan has a place for you too. Maybe you worried that the election of an African American president would cause you to disappear in a kind of reverse-rapture fashion when, in a puff of smoke, all racists would be gone, leaving only the truly chosen liberals to reign supreme. (This prompted real paranoia in far-left-wingers who feared that, like carriers of a recessive gene, anyone could be a latent racist without knowing it.) Rest easy: besides a few reports that a handful of people have gone missing, the world is still just as overpopulated as it was before. Most important, you survived!

True, some of your friends and relatives are nowhere to be found. Some who were not ready for change voluntarily relocated to space pods where they ponder the paradox of progress as they safely orbit the earth. Others can be reclaimed after ninety days in one of the post-racism rehabilitation centers run by the gentle but firmly transformative Dr. Drew.

What's That Smell? Breathe It In!

The fresh feeling of Obamistan greets you like the wafting aroma of your grandmother's traditional stuffed apple pancakes served with the contemporary flair of a triple skinny soy chai mocha latte. It is the sweet-smelling blend of the new and old ways coming together in perfect harmony. You don't have to let go of the things you love about the past in order to embrace your future. Like a finely

NEW!
and improved!

aged wine, Obamistan enhances a complex body of familiarity with a clean note of progress.

Step out your front door and breathe the new racism-free air. Take this slowly—one step and one breath at a time. It is going to blow your mind—like that time you went to the oxygen bar. Remember how addictive that was? It made it hard to breathe "regular" air afterward. The good news is that now racism-free air *is* the regular air. It is healthy, clean, and plentiful, but be careful—all that clarity is a bit of a shocker at first.

If stepping outdoors is too much, you might start by peeking your head out your screen door or cracking the nearest operable window. Hey, where did those security bars go? They are gone, silly. You don't need your paranoia-induced iron barricade anymore. This is the land of racial harmony. You don't have to be afraid of entire groups of people, and you don't have to be afraid of the police. You don't even have to be afraid of the criminals! With racial profiling now ended, the cops focus all of their energy on catching the real perpetrators, and crime rates have decreased significantly.

Once you have taken that first breath, go for it! Open all the doors and windows fully and let the sweet Obamistani air stream into your lungs, your home, and your life! Can you feel the love?

Now that you are acclimated to the tension-free air, go ahead and take your first full step outside. It's safe. Do you notice anything right away? Does the sky seem clearer? That's right. Pollution levels have also decreased. Racism was an eco-crisis in its own right.

If you are a person of color, take an extra deep breath. You will notice that that nasty, phlegm-filled, persistent cough that your doctor could never diagnose, let alone cure, has completely cleared up. Ever wondered why asthma rates were so high in the black population? It was not genetics; it was racism. Doctors in Obamistan are reporting that the number of asthmatics is dropping daily. People are throwing their inhalers out the window. The fall of racism reached places you never imagined.

Now that you can breathe a bit easier, put on your favorite outfit and get ready to take on the world. Your first stop hasn't changed. It is time to visit the cute barista at the corner coffee shop for your morning coffee. Hey, why not take it black today? You have always wondered how black tastes, and now you can try a sip or two without any hint of racial metaphor. Does it taste kind of bitter? That's OK. No one will think you are a racist for spitting it out. Go ahead—add as much cream as you want. You won't be accused of "whitewashing" or trying to "lighten up" your world. Coffee really is just coffee, and everything in Obamistan is delicious.

Help!

Are you feeling alone in this brave new world? Are some of the changes taking you by surprise? It's OK to need a little support adjusting to Obamistan. There are plenty of ways to find the help you need.

Log On: Obamistan is fully functioning in Web 2.0. Besides the national Web site and Facebook page, a lively Twitter feed will give you up-to-the-second information about your new country in 140 characters or less. You'll get breaking news, quirky tidbits, and of course, the most trivial and mundane details. People have clicked to find fun status updates like "Obamistan is chillin' with South Africa and Germany at the UN conference on racism" or "Pop the champagne, y'all! Obamistan just brokered peace between Palestine and Israel!" And even this: "Another boring day in the most perfect country in the world." Follow it all @realobamistan. Don't fall for the posers.

Tune In: If you prefer a more human interface, tune in every week to your local public radio station to hear about people just like you exploring life in your new country. "This Obamistani Life" brings you "poignant and witty audio illustrations of both regular and complicated folks courageously navigating their everyday existence with a dash of kitsch while they search for the meaning of life and universal understanding" (*Obamistan Times*).

Dial Up: Finally, there are several help lines to get you through moments of crisis:

- ➤ 1-800-OBAMA-4U is the official Obamistan Help Center.
- ➤ 1-866-WTF-OBMA is handling general confusion and concerns.
- ➤ 1-888-FU-OBAMA "We want Old America back!"
- ➤ There is also 1-800-HOT-MESS where you can phone in your gripes about news, fashion, Hollywood, or anything else.

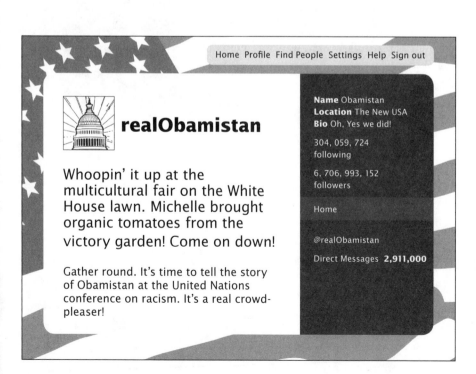

Home Profile Find People Settings Help Sign out

realObamistan

Name Obamistan
Location The New USA
Bio Oh, Yes we did!

304, 059, 724
following

6, 706, 993, 152
followers

Home

@realObamistan

Direct Messages **2,911,000**

Whoopin' it up at the multicultural fair on the White House lawn. Michelle brought organic tomatoes from the victory garden! Come on down!

Gather round. It's time to tell the story of Obamistan at the United Nations conference on racism. It's a real crowd-pleaser!

Oh snap! RT @coolcolin @classycondi: Told you that be-atch was a lunatic. Hatching a plan for the Dems to take us in. Unpack your high-heeled boots.

Gotta run! Jetting to the Israel-Palestine Museum of Lasting Peace to judge the annual flatbread bake-off. Yum!

The girls are loving their new school! RT @obamababes: Quaker meeting is awesome! We love doing community service. It's just like home!

Got health care? You do now! Time to fix those broken teeth and get that dislocated toe reset. Go and get yourself healed—the tab is on us.

RT @BigWillyStyles: Watch out, Germany! Hillary is working on her suntan to give Angela Merkel a run for her money, Obama-style. My girl wants a country of her own to run!

Trending Topics
Universal Health Care
Nuclear Non-proliferation
Henry Louis Gates
NBA Playoffs
G20
Approval Rating
SNL

What's It All About,
Obamistan?

Almost everything has morphed with the changing of the color guard. Sometimes you will feel like a stranger in a strange land. Do you need help navigating the ups and downs of this fresh new terrain? *Obamistan! Land without Racism* is your user's manual. With this guide in hand, you will discover where to pay the white tax, how to get your reparations check, where to welcome your family as they cross the border, what happened to that crazy racist uncle of yours, and much more. Are you ready? Turn the page and get your Obamistan on!

Accents

....

A Testimonial by Su Yin

I swear I am about to cry as I write this. I really thought
this day would never, ever come—not in my lifetime, not
in the lifetime of the kids I hope to have one day, not in the
lifetime of the grandkids I hope to have one day. But today
that day finally arrived.

My whole life I have heard people make fun of the
way they think Asians and Asian Americans talk. People
have been harassing me with "ching chong" for ages in
school, offices, and on TV (shout-out to Rosie O'Donnell,
Al Roker, and Kathie Lee Gifford).

On top of that, when I told people that I was Taiwan-
ese, people used to act surprised that I was not a plastic
doll, since that's the only thing they knew of, that came
from Taiwan. Then they would say, "You mean, you're
Chinese," as if Taiwan were a gated community in the

suburbs of Shanghai. It felt like a miracle when someone actually knew about Taiwan, let alone understood the historical struggle between it and China.

But today . . . *today* I woke up in Obamistan where I will never have to hear "ching chong" again. I will never be told, "You speak such good English!" No one will speak loudly and slowly to me assuming that I am an illiterate, illegal freeloader instead of a summa cum laude graduate of an Ivy League university whose family has been here for generations.

I pinch myself every day wondering if it is real. Even better, my biological clock has gone off permanent snooze. Now that there's one less terrible thing my kids will have to face in this world, I think I might even start a family.

Acting White

••

For decades people of color were kept outside of mainstream success by the charge, "You are acting white" and the guilt that this phrase imposed. Many held themselves back from academic excellence in an attempt to portray themselves as authentic members of their racial group. Some refused to speak proper English or learn English at all. This made Bill Cosby furious. Brown-skinned boys and girls across the nation hid their country music CDs under their mattresses and behind their Ludacris posters. They joined Internet communities where they used code names to find other people "like them." Young virtuosos of color practiced viola and oboe secretly in their closets, while in public they spewed gangsta rap lyrics and strained their necks carrying oversized boom boxes. Kids who could have been Pulitzer Prize-winning poets and journalists spent their days practicing adding -izzle to the ends of words.

The good news is that in Obamistan white people no longer corner the market on being smart, studious, wealthy, well spoken, or sophisticated. The bad news is . . . well, depending on who you are, that might be bad news.

This should be liberating for Bobby Jindal, who seems to have forgotten that he can be a conservative, straight-up nutso Republican and still keep his Indian name. Now that's progress!

Adoption

....

Toward the end of Old America, there was a growing adoption crisis. So many needy kids were being passed over in favor of trendy and affordable foreign babies. Many children of color in need of homes were left wandering the streets only to be picked up by welfare-seeking foster parents. This prompted international outrage and response. After Bono held a benefit concert titled "Orphan Aid," white Europeans began to adopt Old American children of color in droves. So many Europeans adopted brown Old American babies that Angelina Jolie's brood started to look like the Partridge Family. The streets, foster homes, and adoption agencies in Old America were virtually emptied of children of color in a matter of months. Formerly unwanted Old American children now had posh lives in regal homes in gracious countries full of wine, cheese, art, and music. The kids loved it.

That's what really got the attention of Old Americans, who hated being outdone by Europeans. Of course, the New Americans—Obamistanis—wanted little Malias and Sashas to call their own. How dare the Europeans take what rightfully belongs here at home! Since the formation of Obamistan, cross-racial, in-country adoptions have doubled. It is rumored that it is harder to get on waiting lists for brown-skinned Obamistani babies than the lunch list at Spago. The demand is so great that some Latino and black Obamistani families have started adopting the white children who have been left behind.

African American or Black?

You remember this one. This was a constant conundrum in Old America: what do we call the darkies?

Black is beautiful! Black power! Many Old Americans felt that the word *black* was a word of pride. Others, tired of being compared to the grim reaper, spam, communists (blacklists), extortion (blackmail), and sins on the souls of Catholics, felt like it was a dirty word tantamount to an insult. In the face of inconsistent messaging by black . . . err . . . African American people, who couldn't agree on what they wanted to be called, it was absolute mayhem. White people were even heard using *black* as a noun, similar to an object like a shoe or a profession like a mechanic: "You're a black" or "I love you blacks." People just didn't know what to do with the word. It is a wonder the country elected a black . . . African American . . . half-black . . . biracial . . . white-mamma-having-but-still-black-err-African American dude at all.

In Obamistan people know that a wide range of dark-skinned people can have a black experience in this country without having ever set foot on a slave ship. Jamaican English, Barbadian Germans, even some Puerto Ricans have a black experience, though none of them are African American. Obamistanis get the "both and" thing.

Airports

....

A Testimonial by Pardeep

I am *loving* Obamistan! It has made airplane travel so much easier. Flying used to be easy for me but then 9/11 and all. Shout-out to all my black friends. I know you didn't have it easy before the whole terrorism thing went down, but since then, all laser eyes have shifted focus from black to brown. In Old America I had to get to airports an extra hour or two early to allow for interrogation time. Every time I flew to Ohio for a family gathering I would get asked, "Where are you *really* going?" Then my ticket would be flagged for "special search," which could take an unpredictable amount of time depending on how many times I had to rewrap my turban. Then I'd end up being manually scanned by some guy with a baseball-bat-shaped wand because I couldn't take off my kara. They seemed to think it was some kind of weapon. (I don't know how to kill someone with a bracelet, do you?) I don't even want to talk about what they'd do to my beard. A few times I rented a car instead. It was actually faster than flying.

But *now* . . . I sail right through! In fact, last time I flew, the TSA looked at my boarding pass, called me by name—with a *Mr.* in front of it!—cautioned me to stay warm because Ohio was having a rough winter, and waved me through when my kara set off the metal detector. "No worries," said the attendant. "Bole so nihal! Have a good visit with your family. Make sure you come back, though. We'd miss you if you were gone for too long."

American Indian

....

Ah, the story of Old America . . . A courageous and adventuresome explorer named Columbus strikes out for the subcontinent but ends up—*whoops!*—miraculously stumbling onto a "new world" where scores of his future progeny would be sure to prosper. The only glitch was the tons of people already living there. Columbus, ever faithful to his poor navigation skills, called these people "Indians" since India was where ol' Columbus was headed anyway. He probably figured that it wouldn't matter what he called the people he found living there since they would soon be extinct.

One of Columbus's many legacies is that the term *Indian* is pretty darn confusing. For the record, there is an actual country named India that is full of actual Indians. Some of these people even live in the United States and call themselves *Indian American*, which gets readily confused with the term *American Indian*, which evolved from Columbus's misnomer. This caused Old Americans to think and say some wacky things in their failed attempts to distinguish between the two groups: "What kind of Indian?" "Do you mean a giant-diaper Indian like Gandhi or a bow-and-arrow Indian like Tonto?" At their worst, some people would ask, "Spot or feather?" Old Americans loved to reduce racial identity to kitschy sound bites.

In Obamistan, people have actually figured out that indigenous North American peoples are not from India. Correct: Columbus did not actually land in India. It only follows that the people he found here are not Indians. You will find that *Indian* is used to identify people who are from the country of India or have Indian heritage. Conversely Obamistanis honor the people who were here when the country was colonized by using the term *First Americans*. Obamistanis, ripe to get credit for their historic first of ending racism, are quick to acknowledge any other group that deserves props for its own "first" credit.

Animal Mascot:
The Wandering Albatross

....

It is time to bury the old bird. The bald eagle is an unmistakably regal and powerful creature, but Obamistan wanted a new, fresh mascot to go with its new, fresh attitude. The bald eagle's white head, holding its intelligence superior atop the laboring limbs of its brown body, did not sit well with the newfound passion for equality that marks the Obamistani spirit. Plus the eagle has a nasty habit of gouging out the eyes of its rival birds, an image Obamistan was eager to shed. Obamistan is a country with a sensitive soul, a broad reach, a commitment to all it has lost and won over the course of history, and an all-over speckled coloring.

The new animal mascot for Obamistan is . . . the wandering albatross.

At first glance, this might seem like a truly odd bird to represent the country known as the leader of the free world, but allow yourself to dig deeper—that is the Obamistani way. The wandering albatross has the largest wingspan of any living bird, up to between 251 and 350 cm (Obamistan finally switched to the metric system). Though such wide wings can cast a cold shadow over anyone in the vicinity of the bird, Obamistanis prefer to view this as a symbol of Obamistan's willingness to welcome everyone and anyone under its brown and white feathers.

The wandering albatross is an industrious arctic bird, able to withstand a variety of climates, a fact that evokes Obamistan's ability to emerge from the long, cold period of its racist history. It is equally light and dark in color; this symbolism alone speaks volumes. It mates for life. Once Obamistan has become your ally, it will have your back until the very end. When picking a mate, the bird does a famous sky-pointing dance in which it waddles around and thrusts its beak upward over and over again, puncturing the sky with its determination. Like the bird they have chosen as their mascot, Obamistanis thrust their heads above all others as they work stubbornly toward their most idealistic dreams, no matter how impossible they might seem. It was this trademark tenacity that allowed Obamistanis to conquer racism and establish their fine new country. They are committed to applying that same kind of determination to everything they do, from ending pandemic war to financing those fancy new hybrid SUVs. Obamistanis never worry about how silly they look or how humble they feel when they are aiming for greatness.

The legends and myths about the wandering albatross are a rich part of the Obamistani image. Traditional yarns tell us that this sentimental bird is a symbol for preserving the memory of lost sailors. In tribute to those people who gave their lives in the founding and building of the country and to those who lost their lives around the world in Old America's quest for world domination, Obamistanis proudly display the symbol of the albatross on their uniforms, currency, and all official documents. The plethora of ribbon-shaped magnets that were mutating like viruses on the backs of cars in Old America—in a bumper-sticker stand-off not seen since the Vietnam War—have been replaced as Obamistanis acknowledge their fallen soldiers without resorting to divisive ribbon wars. Images of the new bird please the entire political spectrum. The wandering albatross declares that the stories of those who have died for this country—whether through conquest, genocide, enslavement, overthrow, or being sent off to die at the feet of its enemies—will never be forgotten.

In an effort to protect the bird and exalt its place at the helm of the new land, wandering albatross sanctuaries have popped up all over the country. The National Geographic Channel hosts a daily half-hour show at 5 AM for people to wake up with the bird that guides them. The host of the show offers ways that the habits of the bird can inspire greatness in even the simplest Obamistani citizen. This is followed by *Wandering Albatross Workout*, which really puts your personal wingspan to work. Kids cuddle up with comforting albatross stuffed animals and sleep soundly knowing that their country loves them. Suze Orman's new book, *An Abundant Albatross*, provides great new tools to funnel money into your most heartfelt goals. Ken Burns is working on a feature-length documentary about the albatross due to be released on the next Fourth of July.

Finally, no one can forget the infamous albatross from the poem *The Rime of the Ancient Mariner*, which exemplified the cumbersome and menacing weight of the world. But instead of shooting the albatross with a crossbow, Obamistanis embrace their flawed hero. Obamistanis proudly wear wandering albatross pendants as a reminder that they have lifted the weight of racism from around their necks and therefore can conquer anything. Actors, athletes, and spelling bee champions, tugging tearfully at their pendants, thank the albatross for giving them the strength they need to meet their goals.

A wonderful, rich, and beloved mascot, the wandering albatross prompts Obamistanis to believe that no matter how heavy or awkward the burden of history might sometimes feel, they will be able to spread their wings, point to the sky, come out of the cold, commit for life, and live forever in the legends of the world.

Apologies

··

Here are a few "apologies" that were often overheard in Old America that just won't fly in Obamistan:

"I'm sorry you felt hurt."

"I'm sorry you misunderstood."

"I'm sorry you don't see things my way."

"I'm sorry you got offended."

"I'm sorry I benefited from your genocide and abuse, but there's nothing I can do about it now."

You get the picture. After centuries of weak apologies for the crimes that helped to establish the United States, the country finally realized that admitting responsibility, taking action, and making amends were considerably more effective at healing wounds and bringing the country together as a whole. This emerged naturally after the fall of racism because the country realized that centuries of "I'm sorry for slavery" paled in comparison to giving a black guy the keys to the Oval Office. The country seemed to voice a collective "Oh! So, that is what access to real power means!"

This trickled down to all aspects of Obamistani culture. With reparations checks arriving daily in the mailboxes of people of color and the white tax in full swing, the country had a good wake-up call about the cost of treating each other poorly. Children started to treat each other kindly on the playground for fear that they would have to give their favorite toys to the kids they pushed around. Abusive husbands stopped beating their wives when they realized that it meant women would be entitled to their four-wheelers. Slumlords started fixing up housing units so they would not have to pay for their tenants' groceries for the month. Police knew that they would have to spend a night in the slammer if they arrested someone who simply "looked criminal." It is one of the most exciting results of the fall of racism.

Unfortunately, apology culture was deeply embedded in the Old American psyche. It is going to take some practice to get rid of a few of your old tools and crutches. People just don't trust the words "I'm sorry" anymore. In Obamistan you are more likely to hear someone say, "I understand what I've done, and I will work to make sure I never injure you or anyone else in that way again. Is there anything I can do now or in the future that will help redress this wrong?" It takes a little longer to say, but it does wonders for you and the person you may have hurt.

In fact, the only non-apology you'll hear Obamistanis saying is "I'm sorry we elected the coolest black president in the world and made your country look so boring!"

Pop Quiz: Patriotism

As an Obamistani, I _____.

a) divorce myself from this country and all it has ever stood for, but enjoy all the perks of living here.

b) embrace the new image of my country and forget everything that makes me uncomfortable.

c) scream at my leaders when they don't do what I command them to do, but spend most of my time doing that instead of helping out.

d) can't wait to get to work making this country the best it can be!

Answer: d. Obamistanis are shovel-ready!

Arab

··

Before September 11, 2001, very few Old Americans knew what an Arab was; most thought it was a mythical creature in a turban who could open cave walls with the turn of a phrase. After that date, Old Americans' picture of Arabs was just as flat but far more sinister. The words *Arab* and *terrorist* were as synonymous as *black man* and *drug dealer*, *Latino* and *migrant worker*, or *Asian* and *child prodigy*. When they weren't blaming Arabs for the sudden truncation of their personal freedoms, Old Americans were blaming Arabs for the shortage of oil and high prices at the gas pump.

Old Americans easily forgot that, centuries before this country was even a glimmer in the eye of the colonists, Arabs had invented algebra and created the numerical system used in nearly every corner of the world. You don't have Roman numerals on your calculator, do you? Obamistanis stopped blaming Arabs and started giving them props where props were due.

Asking "What Are You?"

··

Remember when you could barely hear that woman talking to you because your brain was nagging you with "What is she? What is she? What is she?" (The way a puppy watching someone walking with a tennis ball thinks, "Throw the ball! Throw the ball! Throw the ball!") Yeah, distracting. To placate such overactive brains without having to succumb to direct communication, some people would try to subtly steer the conversation toward race, hoping that the ambiguously raced woman might drop a hint about her mysterious brown skin, pale eyes, or thick hair. Even if she were talking about learning the backstroke, Old Americans would find a way to make that conversation about race. "My friend's cousin is black, and he can't swim at all . . . so, what are you?" Or "Isn't the Chinese Olympic diving team amazing . . . so, what are you?" It was getting embarrassing. Many Old Americans did not know how to ask about race or even say *race*. They would dance around the question with a choreographed routine: "What are you? Where are you from? Where are your parents from? Where did they grow up?" Worse still, some pretentious Old Americans would doubt the answer when it was finally received. "Really? You don't look Filipino. Are you sure?" This was Old American racial ineptness at an all-time low.

Often Old Americans referred to race as if it were something that had occurred in the past. "My racial background is . . ." was a phrase commonly heard in Old America. Unfortunately "racial background" sounds more like something you choose at the Sears Portrait Studio than an essential part of your daily reality.

Now when Obamistanis want to know what race someone is, they can inquire without dancing around like a kid who needs to pee or stuttering through it like a botched marriage proposal. They simply ask, "What's your race?", and they believe the answer.

Beauty

··

Women of color will enjoy this one. Remember the rollercoaster ride of "exotic" beauty in Old America? For years you were considered ugly because of your deep brown skin and kinky hair, and then a trendy store put a couple of short-haired, African models in its underwear campaign and virtually overnight being brown and nappy was mysterious, glamorous, and chic. Everyone wanted to date you, know you, or at least be seen with you and your "jungle-like grace." Then a few years later, the advertisers changed tactics. Dark and tight was out, and light and wavy was in. Just like that, you were out of style. To make matters worse, your light-skinned, wavy-haired best friend was getting calls from all the people who used to want to hang out with you. Darn those freaking Gap ads!

In Obamistan trendy ethnic beauty is over. People will no longer tell you "You're so unusual-looking," because you won't be. In Obamistan people have friends and family of all different races, so your "exotic charm" won't be much of a surprise.

Being Yourself

∙∙

People everywhere are discovering their true personalities because they no longer have to represent their entire race. That had become a real drag in Old America. People had stopped trying to know one another and just related to others based on the evening news. After 9/11, Arabs, South Asians, and anyone with a beard were treated as threats to the country's security. After the O.J. Simpson trial, black people had to avoid wearing gloves unless they didn't fit. After Jeffrey Dahmer was arrested for cannibalism, white people had to constantly answer the question, "Are you going to eat me?"

In Obamistan, people will let you be yourself. This may seem like a challenge at first. Many of you have developed some bad habits because your every action was held up as an example of your entire demographic, so give yourself some breathing room. In fact, why not try a few things that you felt you could never do before for fear of shattering (or validating) the myths about your racial group? You can now comfortably eat watermelon in public, shake your booty off beat, excel at math, or even do drugs and commit crimes without your entire race taking the fall (or credit). You will probably gain a couple of new hobbies now that you can do whatever you want. Go ahead and take that country-western line-dancing class you keep eyeing at the studio where you take hip-hop dance. No one is going to call you whitewashed now.

People of color now have to stop saying "good white people" to distinguish the few they can trust from the rest who are out to get them. White people have to stop saying "clean, articulate, and graceful" to identify the few people of color they aren't afraid of. This might be hard, as it requires people to relate to each other with open minds regardless of the color of their skin, the thickness of their accent, or the state of their dental work.

On a more intimate level, being yourself brings a surprising freedom to sexual relationships. Men will find that penis size and sexual prowess are no longer prejudged according to skin color. You will actually have a better shot with women, who will have to get to know you before deciding what you are like in the sack. Women will experience a similar freedom from dating fetishes and assumptions about their sexual tastes based on race. Remember the lyrics from the old Rolling Stones song "Some Girls?": "White girls they're pretty funny . . . Black girls just wanna get fucked all night . . . Chinese girls are so gentle"? Well, you can flush those stale ideas down the toilet with Mick Jagger's leopard stretch pants.

Black

A Testimonial by Ericka

I've noticed that in Obamistan people don't think that *black* is a bad word. When referring to a black person, people no longer whisper "black" like it was a life-threatening disease. Remember how people used to stutter when they tried to say that someone is "buh . . . buh . . . bluh . . . black," often becoming so scared to say the b-word that they stumbled into some other *b* descriptor to put before it, which I suppose made "black" easier to say. Remember? For so many white people, even trying to describe a black man walking down the street was difficult; they would start to say "black" but then get nervous and say something like:

"I saw this buh . . . buh . . . BIG black man walking down the street. Oh, did I say big? I meant beautiful. This . . . buh, buh . . . buh-UTIFUL . . . black man. Yeah, *beautiful*, that is what I meant. I mean, he was *big*, but he was also beautiful."

It would take them so long to get "black" out of their mouths that, by the time they did, they were so traumatized that they forgot why they had brought up the big, beautiful black man in the first place. This precipitated many blank stares from white people; I guess they were waiting for me to either approve or get offended by their descriptions. When I stared back at them, simply waiting for them to finish their sentences, panic often ensued, frequently resulting in the comment "You don't think I'm racist because I said that, do you?" *Awk-ward.*

I also am excited to report that kindergarten and elementary school art teachers have also stopped proclaiming, "Black is not a color!" at the top of their lungs. They recognize that this has confused children for decades and had become a frequent playground taunt used against black children. Ugh! I hated that! Especially when it made its way from the playground of my childhood to the office staff meetings of my adulthood. People really hold on to that stuff they learn as kids. Now the teachers leave the dynamics of color theory for a time when students can understand it (like in art school), and let kids be kids and have fun with their paint.

Black, White, Chinese, You Know . . . Everybody!

··

Yep, that sure is everybody. This peculiar inventory was commonly heard when Old Americans were praising their ability to include all races, but this odd triad sounded more like it belonged in a kindergarten snack-time sing-along: "Everybody we know loves to eat cheese! Everybody we know, black, white, and Chinese!" Sadly, many Old Americans saw the world in terms that even Mother Goose would find remedial. Obamistanis are a bit more grown-up with regard to their racial inventories. In fact, Obamistanis realize that there is no simple way to list "all the races" because race is a complicated, growing, evolving and . . . well, diverse thing.

Cafeterias

••

In Old America, white people used to sit together at tables in cafeterias huddled over food, deep in conversation, or laughing out loud as others passed by. These threatening, exclusionary, conspiring packs menaced college campuses all over the nation, leaving people of color no choice but to sit at tables together. But when they did, all hell broke loose. Panels were convened, with scholars and experts claiming that "people of color are racist too." Special news reports did in-depth investigations into the meaning of the mobs; books were written strategizing about the epidemic of brown-skinned kids simultaneously consuming institutional grub in college dining halls across the nation. It became a national obsession, distracting from the white co-eating phenomenon (and laws) that started the whole thing to begin with.

Obamistanis, having stamped out race-based paranoia, now see how people of similar races, particularly those who have experienced oppression, might have some things to talk about with each other. It's not a big deal; it is just like a knitting circle, except with noodles instead of needles.

Chess

••

Whoa! Put down that white pawn for your e4 e5 opening. In Obamistan the black chess pieces make the first move.

Child Care

··

Had you been nanny-sharing your Jamaican immigrant child-care worker with your entire mommies-on-the-go playgroup? Old Americans loved to pass a person of color around among themselves, especially if it were tax-free. Sure, your nanny earned a living wage—she just had to work for five families to do it.

Obamistanis still value the influence of a wide range of cultures on their children, but instead of achieving this through a revolving door of hired help, they expose their kids to their friends and extended family members. Now when your son calls an older Dominican woman "auntie," it's because she is married to your brother.

Children

....

"I'll tell my children about racism when it comes up naturally." This was the lackadaisical parenting approach taken by so many Old Americans. The thing is, when does racism ever come up "naturally" in a *good* way? Never. Picture it: naive Noah uses the n-word, thinking it just means "stupid"; sincere little Sally pulls her eyelids into slants and bows, saying, "Sayonara"; Tucker teasingly tapes a feather to his head and whoops and hollers as he pretends to scalp his friends; Ingrid innocently asks Raul, "When are you getting deported?" These "natural" moments may have been learning opportunities for white kids, but they really sucked for kids of color.

Fortunately, Obamistani parents talk confidently with their children about race before their precocious little feet naturally step in steaming piles of racism and cause unfortunate incidents at their schools. Children listen with rapt attention as parents expertly explain that "Joseph is white, Harry is African American, and Suzy is Asian American," and how our rich and colorful history makes life fun and exciting. The stress, terror, and avoidance that plagued those conversations before has evaporated. Parents no longer silence their children's curiosity with "Shhh. Honey, it's not polite to talk about that stuff," or "We'll talk about that when you are older." They don't slaughter their children's friends' names or ask at the PTA meeting, "What exactly is your little boy?" Parents no longer pack meals for their kids when they have sleepovers at "different" people's houses, for fear that their children will be fed kung pao dog or curried lizard tail. Happy-go-lucky Obamistani youngsters play with their multi-colored friends with a carefree confidence. With all this new, healthy communication occurring between parents and kids, it is much easier to bring up other important topics such as drugs, sex, guns, and Internet pornography. You know, the hard stuff.

Chocolate

···

For years people of color have worried that white people were going to eat them. This stemmed from the frequency with which white people described people of color as if they were food. While "alabaster" skin evokes a rare and valued treasure, people of color were portrayed as mass-produced, perishable food items, filled with fat and cholesterol, that could be purchased at any corner deli and devoured in one scrumptious swallow.

"A coffee-colored woman walked into the room, drifting on the wafting warmth of a triple espresso latte." "His skin was like a Hershey's kiss melting in the hot African sun, as if it would stick to your fingers with the slightest touch." People, especially creative writers and public radio journalists, thought they were pretty clever; but really they just seemed cannibalistic. Old Americans basically thought that race and food were the same thing; many even viewed themselves as radical integrationists as they gathered their white friends every Friday to "eat Chinese."

Obamistanis don't need to digest each other in single servings. They know that a Tamil looks different from a Punjabi, and a Peruvian from a Guyanese. They get that many races span the range of skin tones. Obamistanis can simply say "light-skinned," "brown-skinned," or "dark-skinned." They've even discovered, by forming relationships with people of different races, that their personality and character traits are what make them truly delicious.

Compliments

....

"Old Americans are awesome. Your cold, ruthless, me-first attitudes are really admirable. It must be so freeing to have such a stunted emotional landscape that you can simply ignore other people's feelings! If only everyone could be more like you!"

Old Americans were masters of the backhanded compliment. People were so good at it that some wondered if Old America required its citizens to take a course in making insults sound like praise. Those of you on the darker end of the race spectrum often heard the following:

"You speak such good English! Where did you learn that?"

"You are different than other people like you. I really appreciate that."

"You are so nice and easy to talk to. I am pleasantly surprised at how comfortable I am with you."

"You are such a hard worker; it must be because of your people's great work ethic."

"How did you understand what I was talking about? That is amazing."

"She runs so fast and gracefully, just like a gazelle."

"I've never met anyone like you who was not smart."

"I've noticed that most people like you have really white teeth."

"I'd hire anyone of your race in a heartbeat!"

"It is so great that they let someone like you into this place."

"You look a lot like that famous person [of your race]—do you know him?"

Most famously, just before the fall of racism, the presidential rival-turned-sidekick, Joe Biden, praised Obamistan's soon-to-be-leader for being clean and articulate. Brother Biden did not seem to recognize that this made it seem as if all other black people were dirty and verbally defective. Even the press's repeated labeling of the new president as the first "viable" black candidate oddly implied that all other black politicians had been kept alive by some external political life-support system, unable to breathe on their own.

After the election, Obamistanis soon realized that the clean, articulate, viable black guy had control of their economy, health care system, social security, and strategic defense. They also quickly figured out that they should start paying real compliments to people of color, or their tax breaks, legislative loopholes, and government pensions might come to an end.

Congress

··

Tune in to C-Span and take a look at your government in action. No, you're not watching BET or Univision. The House of Representatives and the Senate now look and feel like Jesse Jackson's Rainbow Coalition circa 1980. Yep, you just saw two people hug each other. There are black senators, Latino senators, Asian American senators, and First American Senators. There are even some First Hawaiians and multiracial people too. The Obamistani government is a real conglomeration of people from all different walks of life, working together for a common good, and it plans to stay that way.

The Obamistani population now works hard to have the government reflect the population. If it falls short, a state may volunteer to hold its elections a second time; some have even sought to diversify their populations. Vermont's plot to secede and rekindle the confederacy was quickly curtailed. Red states and blue states have all turned into green states, a term coined by the eco-blazing, once-and-always governor of California, Arnold Schwarzenegger, who could never really choose a party anyway—which is OK because the two-party system was simply too "black and white" for Obamistanis. Now the government contains a record thirty-seven parties. The level of decorum on the floor of the Congress is at an all-time high as your elected officials actively solicit the opinions of those they now consider colleagues, not combatants. This plethora of opinions has finally made manifest the inclusive and innovative decision-making intended by the founders of the nation. You can almost hear Alexander Hamilton cheer, "Now that's representative democracy!"

Cultural Co-optation

....

Obamistanis resist the temptation to make life an all-you-can eat buffet of racial tapas. Being in a post-racism country doesn't mean that now everybody can run around wearing wooden clogs, kilts, cheongsams, Afros, bindis, and turbans—especially not at the same time! Yes, some people will try this approach, but they've simply gone overboard. If you are going to learn how to make njera and doro wat, that is great—everyone loves Ethiopian food—but that doesn't mean you can talk to Nigerians and Senegalese as if you are their long-lost cousin.

Currency

One of the most glaring examples of Old America's love affair with racism was the presence of Andrew Jackson on the twenty-dollar bill. Now this crusader of genocide and defier of the Supreme Court has been removed from the nation's most frequently used greenback. He has been replaced by Geronimo, the rebel Chiricahua Apache who fought against American westward expansion and the genocide of indigenous peoples. One look in Geronimo's haunting eyes makes a person pause, causing Obamistanis to be much more conscious about how and where they spend their dollars.

Other currency changes brought enslaved American rebellion leader Nat Turner to the hundred-dollar bill, sharing the stage with Benjamin Franklin. Now people who work hard for their money say, "I'm ballin' for Benji-Nats." Ulysses Grant was booted from the fifty-dollar bill and replaced by Holocaust hero Dr. Feng Shan Ho. The two-dollar bill now sports scenes of the Constitutional congress, African American field laborers, Chinese railroad workers, and Latino farmers. The first Asian American Congressperson, Dalip Singh Saund, is honored on the dime, while the nickel features Ellen Ochoa, the first Latina American astronaut. Abraham Lincoln, though he embodies the true spirit of Obamistan, was taken from the penny since he already had a place on the five-dollar bill. Now the little copper onesies are graced with the face of Albert Einstein, who was an outspoken voice for racial equality. Finally, a three-dollar bill was minted in honor of gay, lesbian, bisexual and transgendered Obamistanis, with RuPaul's perfect smile and shining style winking right at you.

Of course, the Big O himself is on the back of every bill. Each one shows a historic scene of the Obama presidency—the election, the "racism speech," saving the economy, instituting universal health care, planting a victory garden, fending off global viruses, brokering world peace, and, of course, playing basketball with the secretary of education as they reform public schooling nationwide.

Cutting in Line

••

In Old America even small things, like cutting in line or allowing someone to cut in line in front of you, could spark mini race wars. It was not uncommon to hear white people tell people of color, "It is just one person! You will get your turn—just wait!" This only poured salt in centuries-old wounds. People of color felt that racism was flogging them at every turn—even going to the grocery store or the post office could result in a nasty reminder of second-class citizenship. White people felt that the world was harsh and unpredictably violent and never knew when they would be accused of racism by paranoid and delusional people of color. These moments contributed to widespread racial insanity in Old America.

In Obamistan everyone appreciates just how potent a simple gesture can be. White people have made cutting in line a wonderful way to work their racism recovery program, frequently giving up their place in line to people of color, who respond, "You are so generous!" White people reply, "No, you deserve it." This type of exchange was rarely heard in Old America, except in role-playing exercises in interracial marriage counseling. Today, a willingness to share what you have with everyone in your community is a fundamental building block of Obamistani culture.

Dating

A Testimonial by Graciela

Dating is so much better in Obamistan! Wow. So, OK, I got set up on a date with this white dude who is a friend of someone I work with. I didn't want to go out with him, as my track record with white guys is kinda . . . ugly. We do pretty good until he decides to nickname me "mocha" or say how much he's always wanted to devour my "caramel-coated" skin or breaks out the five words of Spanish that he knows to tell me, "You are looking *muy caliente* tonight!" That stuff is just not sexy. And that's just usually the start of the issues.

But I went out on this date. Why not give things a chance? I figure, if a black man can be elected to the presidency of the United States, anything can happen.

Somewhere halfway through the salads, I figured I should just cut to the chase. If he revealed himself to be like the other guys, I could still catch a movie with my girlfriends.

"So, am I the first Latina you've dated?" I ask as I dip a cherry tomato into my side of ranch dressing.

"No, that's silly. What would make you think that?"

"OK, sorry. The second?"

My date launched into a string of tales from his dating history that made me forget all about my cherry tomato, which dangled patiently on my fork as I listened in stunned silence.

"Actually my first girlfriend was South Asian American; then I dated two white women and two Latinas (one was Dominican American and the other was Venezuelan American) and an African American woman. After a few years off—you know, not taking anyone seriously—I dated a First American woman who was older than me, which is why it didn't work out. I still was not ready for a commitment, which she really wanted. I tried but had to admit that I was not mature enough at that time in my life. My last girlfriend was Korean American, but that was long-distance. That was too hard. I just wanted to be close enough to hug her every day. Her parents loved me, though—I make killer kimchee. My ex-fiancée—I finally did become mature enough to settle down—was Mexican American. That is a longer story. I don't think I'm forgetting anyone . . . oh, wait, Sue was black. But I often try to forget her . . . she was psycho."

After that I was speechless. I popped the tomato into my mouth and waved down the waiter to bring me another gin and tonic.

Describing People

···

You might think that living in a post-racism world means you can finally proclaim, "I don't see color!" But before you start running around with a big pink eraser, rubbing away at people's faces, pause for a moment. Do you really want a world full of skinless people? Do you *literally* not see color? Is your car no longer blue? Is your dog no longer a golden retriever? What would a world without color look like? Could you even see things in this world? Did you really buy that expensive high-definition television to watch 1920 by 1080 pixels of gray? No, you didn't. You love color.

Obamistanis love color too. So don't worry—you've got this. You may be surprised at the level of racial clarity that magically came to you when you cast your vote for the black guy. That act alone made you one of the world's foremost authorities on racial variation. You are ready to roll. If you need some practice, though, why not invite a few friends over and turn on that high-def set of yours? There should be plenty of people of color on there now. Point them out and call out their races. See who can guess the right race first! Who can guess twenty correctly in a row? Give out prizes. Obamistan makes race fun in all kinds of new ways.

Dining

People of color, prepare to be served! (No, it's not a subpoena.) That's right—you will no longer have to listen to your stomach grumble while the diners around you get piping hot plates of food delivered to their tables by friendly waitstaff who entertain them with cheerful banter. As emphasized in so many election speeches, even days before the fall of racism, people of color were being ignored at "dining counters" and restaurants across the country. Sadly this was not just a white-on-color phenomenon. It was not uncommon for black people to not get served at Vietnamese restaurants or for Japanese people to be ignored at the local soul food joint. This mayhem of prejudice led to more and more people of color slowly starving while waiting for food at restaurants. A hunger of epidemic proportions caused fights to break out over any bit of food left on the table. Even the smallest pile of cracker crumbs could lead to a full-scale riot.

In Obamistan, people of color get to eat just like white people. It is a feat of equality that many fought for decades to achieve. You will find that the taste of rotisserie chicken, cheese grits, or your favorite—duck liver pâté—served to you in a public restaurant and devoured in open air in front of other people is one of the most liberating aspects of Obamistani culture. White people, who have been enjoying the pleasure of public eating for years, will smile and say, "That tastes good, doesn't it?" And it does. Freedom is a yummy, yummy thing.

Diverse Person

∙∙

White Old Americans had so many euphemisms for referring to people of color, and "diverse person" was a favorite. One reason they resisted the term *people of color* was because they felt so uncomfortable being white. It was not uncommon to hear them desperately exclaim, "If you are a person of color, what does that make me? Nothing?" They threw fits and rages when referred to as "white."

Soon white people began holding white civil rights rallies and crying, "Don't take our color away!" Eventually the numbers at these protests started to dwindle, and it was discovered that white people felt lonely and bored when people of color were not around. Even they couldn't take the blandness of all-white gatherings. But how could they ask people of color to join them without invalidating their own color? They decided that the word *diverse* meant "exciting, new, different, and something we want" and hoped that using it to describe people of color would attract them to previously all-white clubs, organizations, and events. This worked for a period of time in the 1980s, but like hair bands and fluorescent, paint-splattered mesh shirts, its effectiveness faded as people came to their senses.

White Old Americans did not notice that using the term *diverse person*, besides being grammatically incorrect, was tantamount to calling someone "strange," "alien," or "out of place." They pursued these so-called diverse individuals with such fervor that it became obvious that they were most interested in diversifying their social portfolios to enhance their own image. Diversity became a commodity that white people would trade like hedge funds and derivatives. "Get me some of those diverse peoples," many executives were heard saying. Sadly, like the get-rich-quick schemes of the stock market, all this grabbing at diversity ended up causing a meltdown in the system. Talk about a Great Depression! The diverse individuals didn't make white people feel better at all. They asked white people to examine racism in their language, policies, and actions. This was more than the white people had bargained for. They grew tired and irritable, but ultimately they ran out of people of color, as the three they trusted became overbooked with requests. In the end, people of color withdrew their investments, leaving white people to appeal to the government for a bailout.

Thankfully, Obamistanis are better at race relations, grammar, and investing. In addition, white Obamistanis are much more comfortable with being white and are no longer afraid of feeling lonely and left out of the people-of-color club. They realize that white is all right. If you hear people in Obamistan seeking a "diverse person," feel free to bring them into modern times. Correct them on their grammar and their racial information. You might also want to see if they are still listening to music on cassette tapes and introduce them to MP3s.

Driving Around

....

A Testimonial by Latisha

My sister came to visit to celebrate the dawn of Obamistan and try out the new post-racism ways. She and I had spent hours in Old America kvetching about racism in our jobs and in dating, as well as among our friends and the general public. So we thought we'd do something fun since racism was over. She is a real queen diva, so she insisted that I take her shopping in the ritziest part of town. I'd never actually been there, so I told her to look up the stores on Google Maps. She had a list where she wanted to shop: Tiffany, Coach, bebe, Saks, and a host of other small, high-end boutiques.

"It looks like most of these are all on the same street. Yeah! One long strip of shopping delight!" my sister said with an ear-to-ear grin on her face as she peered at my computer while simultaneously fastening her diamond tennis bracelet.

"OK," I said with a deep sigh as I plowed through my closet to find something that my sister would deem appropriate to wear to such places. "How do we get there?"

"Well, from what it looks like on the map, Martin Luther King Jr. Boulevard goes right to that area of town."

"That's funny, Kamesha—try again."

"No, I'm not kidding. Look at the map. MLK Boulevard goes right there."

"You are just being foolish." I pushed my sis aside and had a look at the map myself. Sure enough, there was MLK Boulevard running through the entire city directly to the wealthy area of town. And get this: the parallel boulevard was named Malcolm X Way! I followed MLK a bit further beyond the shopping district to where the houses were, and as my finger ran through the map it crossed Yuri Kochiyama Avenue, Edward Said Street, and Frida Kahlo Way. I nearly fell over.

"I told you," Kamesha cooed. "See, our people lead the way to exactly where I want to go. Let's hit the stores!"

We hopped into the car, and as I was driving, I was amazed to see MLK Boulevard. There was no trash and no ugly, chipped, and graffitied "uplifting" murals of people rising out of poverty. Instead there were clean, well-kept bronze statues of each person the streets were named after. People of all shades were milling in and out of beautiful houses and fancy stores, carrying bags filled with treasures. I felt like I was in the Emerald City.

Drug Dealers

....

Not only upstanding citizens need a guide to Obamistan. If you are a drug dealer wondering how the changes will affect your business, this section is for you.

First off, if you are a drug dealer of color and are ready to move on to other work opportunities, you should check out the MBA program at your local university. Having already proven your entrepreneurial skills, you will be given a full scholarship. You will probably drop out before you complete your degree, but as in the tradition of Harvard Business School, that will be because you have been offered a fantastic position at a successful firm. This will leave lots of job openings in your former field for white drug dealers to get their start. However, if you are a white drug dealer, you will need to take more serious precautions against arrest. Before, you could just hide behind a copy of the *New York Times* and watch as the cops cuffed and booked the brown-skinned man across the street. But your skin no longer serves as your get-out-of-jail-free card. You won't get less time or lighter sentences either. Basically, the free ride on the white horse is over.

The upside of all of this is that now people are much more aware that you are available to sell them drugs. White drug dealers were getting very frustrated standing on street corners watching their potential clients, time and time again, ask the black kids with the baggy jeans, "Where can I get some of that fire?" Now everyone knows that white people have the fire too. This has resulted in an increase in customers, profits, and overall visibility. It's a real boon for the drug industry.

You will also find that your neighborhoods have a bit more traffic from people seeking drugs for sale. People in Obamistan realize that they can get drugs just about anywhere—not just in the ghettos (which don't exist anymore anyhow)—so you will find that your kids and your kids' friends no longer have to stray far from home to get the drugs they seek.

Drug Sentencing

B2   *local***news**   3

Local Man Sentenced to Life in Prison

Three-strikes powder cocaine law puts another societal menace behind bars.

A routine traffic stop for multiple violations led to drug charges against the man driving a silver Volvo C30 last Friday afternoon on Route 187. A search turned up a can of tire sealant with a hidden

Mike Johnson, 28, was warned several times by the police to cease and desist using and carrying powder cocaine.

compartment. Inside were four plastic bags of a substance that appeared to be powder cocaine. Another bag was found stuffed between the driver's seat and the driver's side door. Police say the driver, Mike Johnson, 28, of Lindyville, had over $2,100 in cash and two postal money orders totaling $1,200.

The suspect was held on various charges including possession with intent to deliver. A routine background check revealed that Johnson had two prior arrests for transporting powder cocaine, making this his third. This put the state's three-strikes law into effect for Johnson, who was sentenced immediately to life in prison.

See DRUGS p. 13

Emotions

....

A Testimonial by Vincent

It was nearly impossible for me to express my emotions publicly in Old America. I nearly went nuts trying to hold my feelings in and then blowing my stack when I couldn't take any more. My wife used to complain that I was turning into a cold, unfeeling block of ice some days and a complete volcano on others. Even something as simple as trying to order a birthday cake could put me on the verge of losing it. For my niece's twelfth birthday, we put in an order with our grocery store for a chocolate cake with an image of a beautiful blue mountain. She loves hiking and chocolate, and blue is her favorite color. The cake decorator got the chocolate frosting right, but the mountain was this oddly shaped, olive green blob, topped with pale yellow streaks, which looked more like a pile of puke than an inspiring mountain peak. Anyone would have been upset about this. I calmly pointed this out to the person behind the bakery counter and asked if he could redo the cake in time for the party at four. He looked positively terrified. "OK, OK! Don't pull out a Samurai sword on me or anything! We'll fix it!"

While I was waiting, the manager of the bakery came out and said, "Sir, I heard we had a problem with your order. There's no need for you to get heated. We're not prejudiced; we just got the order wrong." *Who had said anything about prejudice?* She continued, "My staff tells me that you are a black belt in karate. We don't want to have any problems. Maybe you can just meditate or do some Tai Chi for a few minutes while we fix your cake." I may have been calm at first, but by then I was pissed. White people in Old America often wondered why people of color were always so angry. They rarely figured out that it was probably because of something they did.

Anyway, Obamistan is much better. Now, I can complain and bitch and moan all I want, and no one thinks I am starting a race war or going to break out in a tantrum of Wing Chun. But even more exciting, I simply don't get as angry as I used to. My wife is much happier, and so am I. Leaving all that racial tension behind has done more for my sense of inner peace than any amount of Tai Chi could have ever done.

Family

In Old America things were getting pretty out of hand with regard to familial lines. People would willy-nilly call each other "bro" and "sis" without the slightest bit of consideration as to whether their new bro was actually related to them, liked them, or even knew them. It was especially irritating to people of color, who were often the targets of these drive-by adoptions. In Obamistan your actual family is likely to be more colorful, so you won't have to create a grab-and-go family by calling random strangers "uncle" and "cuzz." Inspired by the African-white-Hawaiian-Indonesian family at the head of the country, many Obamistani families shook their family trees and found a few lychees and mangos among the apples. In Old America most families had some form of racial "mystery meat" lurking in their genealogical pantries, but few would admit it openly. Now might be a nice time to sit down with grandma and find out about that long-lost love of hers or ask a certain family friend why your cousin looks so much like him.

FEMA Trailers

....

A Testimonial by Sandra

I called my cousin in New Orleans yesterday to see how Obamistan was treating her, and she told me that the government showed up yesterday and took away all the FEMA trailers. I thought, *Damn! Even* this *government is trying to slowly kill those folks in NOLA.* It has been many years since Hurricane Katrina, and still people are living in shacks and catching unnamed diseases from all the mold and bacteria floating around there. I was about to go off, but before I could start my rant, my cousin stopped me.

"No, no, Sandra, it's not like that anymore. Don't you know they came down here with a slew of help? The National Guard, AmeriCorps, some unaffiliated volunteers, even the Peace Corps came home for a few days, and now we have beautiful new houses to live in. And we *own* them! Yep, they gave us the deeds and affordable mortgages too. Oh, and puppies! I am not kidding. Everyone who got a new house—and that was everyone—was given a dog to bring instant life to the new place. You have to come visit! Come for a dip in the pool! They also built a new school and outfitted it with the latest books and technology. They brought teachers from the best districts in the country to teach the kids. The place has really taken a turn for the real."

Excited but suspicious, I asked, "What did they do with all the moldy gross FEMA trailers? Where are they taking them next?" I was thinking about the next community of color to be dumped on or penned up in the mobile death traps.

"They are recycling them!" she said. "I hear they're going to be eco-friendly shopping bags now."

Food

· ·

You already know that Obamistan has a rekindled love affair with linguistic accuracy. So it will be no surprise that, when you go to a restaurant that serves any of the plethora of Obamistani foods, people will now describe it as an "ethnic *food* restaurant" rather than an "ethnic restaurant." For example, Obamistanis now say "Mexican food restaurant" rather than "Mexican restaurant." This is a simple courtesy to explain to people that you will not be eating actual Mexicans in the establishment, but rather consuming food that originates from Mexico. The distinction might seem small, but it has a big impact. A "burrito place" is a place that sells burritos. Referring to a "Mexican place" gives the same impression— Mexicans for sale—not nearly as tasty. Quick review: You can buy and eat a burrito; you cannot (legally) buy and eat a Mexican.

Other changes include schools no longer serving Black History Month soul food lunches, which were so laden with pork that even Malcolm X would have had to pack a lunch that day. The ever-present Chinese New Year lunch of bean sprouts over canned Chun King noodles has also been retired. It was getting so embarrassing that the Chinese kids and the black kids were bringing their own lunches on those days but eating them secretly so as to avoid questions about their authenticity. In the same vein, adults have stopped thinking that green beer has anything to do with being Irish and have stopped using the fifth of May as an excuse to get drunk on tequila.

Pop Quiz: Eats

I love to eat _____.

a) Mexican

b) Chinese

c) Italian

d) food

Answer: Unless you have become a cannibal, the correct answer is d. Obamistanis like to eat food not people.

Foreclosures

A Testimonial by Dabiku

My mortgage company called today. When I saw the number pop up on the screen of my cell phone, I had to pause for a moment. Usually I would have panicked and pressed the little red phone icon marked "ignore"; but a lot has changed, and I thought that maybe this would be different too. So I nervously pressed the green phone icon marked "answer."

Let me back up a second here. I am a thirty-eight-year-old musician and freelance journalist. I am single and have a dog. I have no one to help me fix a flat tire, let alone help me buy a house. I'd never borrow the tens of thousands of dollars friends of mine have borrowed from their parents for housing down payments. My parents don't have that kind of money anyhow. I haven't had health insurance in twelve years. The one year I made enough money to pay for coverage, Blue Cross turned down my application. I work hard. I live modestly. I have a good education and am damn smart. Still, when I went to sign the documents for my subprime mortgage loan, I was distracted by the Patriot Act disclosure and didn't read all the fine print.

It was my first house. At the time that I bought it, I was pressuring my boyfriend into moving across the country and setting up a life together—house, dog, truck, and all. Three months later, we had split up, and I was a single, self-employed new homeowner with a blind adopted rescue dog and a mortgage made for two. Three years later, the economy started to tank and my bread-and-butter work contracts along with it. My income dropped by 50 percent. Today, I am about two months away from foreclosure, having begged, borrowed, and busted my ass to keep my head above water and my house from "accidentally" burning to the ground the way some people are setting their SUVs on fire to cash in on insurance settlements and get out of the payments.

So, back to the phone call. I took a deep breath.

"H . . . hello?"

"Hello, is this Der-boo-kwah?"

Not *exactly,* I think to myself, all too familiar with the butchering of my name by credit collectors. "Yes, this is she."

"Hi!" I have to hold the phone away from my ear a few inches because the woman on the other end is so enthusiastic and loud. "Oh, it's so good to get in touch with you! This is Fran from Cedarbrook Loan Services. How are you doing today?"

"I'm OK. How are you?" She sounds oddly upbeat. Usually creditors have that pathetic or pissed tone that says, "What excuse am I about to hear now?"

"Well, I am just loving the sunshine outside my window—it's just divine. Plus I am having a great day today helping homeowners with those nasty little subprime loans. How is everything at the house today? How is your little doggie . . . what is her name?"

"Trixie. She's good. Still blind." I wondered how on earth she remembered that I had a dog. It was almost like I was an actual person to her, not just an overdue account.

"Ohhh, bless her heart! She *is* blind, isn't she? Well, I am going to pop a dog treat in the mail with your next statement, I sure am. Just you wait and see."

"Uh, thanks. So, what's up, Fran?" I wanted to cut to the bullying, condescension, and pressuring that usually comes when I answer a call from an 800 number.

"Oh, well, are you a bit nervous? I imagine so. It was so terrible calling people before the election. The whole 'We're coming down hard on the blacks and Latinos' thing was a real bummer."

"What are you talking about?"

"Well, you know, the whole 'subprime for the subhuman' thing. You probably read about it in *Newsweek*, right? The banks couldn't wait to get people of color like you into crappy home loans so that foreign investors could have a field day betting for or against whether you would default on your impossible-to-pay mortgages. The whole 'credit default swap' thing was basically a day at the races for high powered traders, except with desperate homeowners in place of ponies."

"Really?" Here I thought I had been lucky to get my loan and a failure for not being able to keep up with it. Even when the economy crashed and my own bank was bailed out of its defaults, my mortgage company had left me harrowing phone messages and intimidating (and bilingual) notices on my door.

"Yep. It was riotously entertaining for them for a while, but when racism fell, they knew the party had come to an end and that they'd better quickly invent a program to make it all look like a big mistake."

"Oh, really?"

"Yes, *really*. And that's why I am calling you today!"

"Great, Fran. Lay it on me." My plummeting salary and looming foreclosure had not stopped me from being friendly and polite to the people threatening to kick me out on the street.

"Alright, Du-blu-kee, here you go. Oh, first let me get the bank executive on the phone. He's going to explain it all to you firsthand, just like he should have when he gave you that ridiculous mortgage three years ago."

"OK." There was a pause and some clicking as if a third person was entering onto a conference call.

"Hello. Hello? Fran, can you hear me?" Here comes the suit and tie.

"Yep, Stan, you're on!"

Great, Stan and Fran. I felt like I was in the middle of a terrible sitcom pilot. I expected Ashton Kutcher to jump out at any moment and tell me I'd been punk'd.

"Ahem . . ." Stan cleared his throat. This was a good sign. It was the sound of a white man about to part with a large sum of his money.

"Hello, is this Doo-booooo-kee?"

"Yes, Stan. This is Dabiku." Apparently Fran and Stan had not yet had their sessions at the people-of-color name-pronunciation clinic.

"Well, first let me say hello! It is so good to finally meet you. I'm sorry that when our bank gave you your mortgage loan we never took the time to assess your situation thoroughly, find out who or what you were, or if you had any ability to handle the load of money we were about to offer you and then demand that you repay threefold."

"O . . . kay . . ." Was this an apology or . . .

"That's correct, right?" Stan continued. "No one met you or asked you any questions about your income, history, credit, or future, did they?"

"Nope."

"And you used 'stated income' to verify your ability to pay?"

"Yep." *Stated income* basically meant that someone said, "Do you have income?" And I stated, "Sure do!"

"And they signed you up for the blackie . . . uh, *African American* program, right?"

"Well, they said that my brokers were very interested in helping black people achieve the dream of home ownership."

"Right, right, that sounds like the script. And when your broker showed you the paperwork, how long did you have to read the twenty-five pages of legal-size documents that you were signing?"

"About ten minutes."

"And your loan had no down payment?"

"Right."

"And no payment on the principal—interest only?"

"Right."

"And in five years your interest rate was going to 'adjust,' and your payments were going to nearly double, right?"

"No, I didn't sign up for that one."

"Oh, we couldn't get ya there, huh? Smart cookie . . . smart, smart. But your payments are spread out over two mortgages on that house, not just one, making the whole bill even higher, right?"

"Right."

"Yeah, that one was Jack's idea. Heh." Stan muttered under his breath, "And we all just crossed our fingers and figured the housing market would continue to balloon like Pamela Anderson's breasts, and in a few years you'd sell your house for double the money, and then we'd slide you a fat loan for a bigger house in a chic new neighborhood, right?"

"Yep, that sounds like what everyone told me."

"OK, well, you are perfect for our program."

That sounded like what they had said three years ago when I was told that banks loved to lend to first-time homeowners, especially if they were Latino or African American. Needless to say, I was skeptical.

"Needless to say, I am sure you are skeptical," Stan said in an eerie telepathic moment. "I know that in the Old American HELPing Homeowners Program we told you that in order to refinance your home you would have to prove your income and forecast a surplus in your monthly expenses—even though to get into the loan in the first place you didn't have to do that—and that you'd have to make improvements on the home and continue to live there regardless of the decline in the property value."

"Yeah," I said, "but that is impossible. I can't prove my income any more now than I could three years ago. I am a self-employed independent contractor."

"Right! It's entrepreneurship like yours that is the lifeblood of the American . . . I mean, Obamistani economy."

"So I'm told."

"Well, why don't we start rewarding that instead of torturing you with harassing phone calls? My boss and I have gotten plenty bored of flying around the country in private jets, downing bottles of expensive champagne, chanting 'Cheers to the mud people!', and just wondering which there are more of: the stacks of money in our safes or the stars we see out the windows at forty thousand feet?"

"Uh . . . mud people?"

"Oh, sorry. That was internal lingo. I'm sure you read about it in the *Times* article about the pending lawsuit. People are really overreacting—it's just an affectionate pet name for you people who don't pay your bills. Anyway, where was I? Oh, right, on the jet. Well, we won't be living that lifestyle anymore. Someone's got to pay for those crap loans we handed out like dip samples at the grocery store. Anyone involved in creating these garbage mortgages either got fired or had their bonuses withheld. That freed up millions of dollars. Add that to the surplus created when the banks got rid of their predatory loan departments and—*badda-bing!*—now there are plenty of funds to make the situation right for you and the thousands of others like you. So, will you let us make it right?"

I am silent. Putting my trust in these smooth talkers got me into this mess. Plus I think Stan might be a wing nut.

"Listen, we want you to stay in your house. We *really* want you to pay back every penny of your loan. We are out to create a win-win scenario here."

"OK, keep talking."

"And we realize that in Obamistan we can't treat people of color like roosters in a cockfight that battle to the death only to have their carcasses served up in a Sunday night feast for our extended families . . ."

"Uh . . ."

". . . so, here's what we are going to do for you, Dabi-kah. We are going to give you a standard mortgage at an affordable interest rate and consolidate your two mortgages into one. That'll lower your astronomical monthly payment . . . Plus we'll knock off a quarter of the loan so that you can actually have some built-in equity and feel like your home is a real investment instead of a rusty two-ton anchor around your neck, dragging you down into a watery grave. Wouldn't it be nice to eat out every once in a while? We'd love for you to have a bit of extra money to spend patronizing the businesses in your community."

I hadn't paid for a meal at a restaurant in three years. That sounded amazing.

"OK, well . . . what do you need from me?" It sounded so good, but I'd heard offers like that before, and in Old America, most homeowners like me who were in trouble didn't qualify for any of the supposed rescue programs. I figured I would need to produce ten years of tax returns, fifty pay stubs, and a letter from my dead grandmother vouching that she'd sell her coffin on Craigslist if I defaulted.

"Not a thing, Dabiku. We are just calling today to let you know that we've already converted your loan and that your new statements will reflect the changes I've listed. In addition I've been recording this conversation for documentation and will send you a copy so that if ever you have difficulty with us or any other mortgage broker, you can confirm that you have an unbreakable vow from yours truly that we will make sure you stay in your home. Your official confirmation number is 1554432."

"Wow, really?" Now I was letting my guard down, I have to admit. A few tears rolled down my cheeks, and I squeezed my dog tight. If this were true, I could go grocery shopping and fill up two, maybe three, shelves in the fridge, as opposed to the usual one and a half.

"Yes, it's true, Dabiku. Do you agree to the terms?"

Not usually a fan of that phrase, I checked in again. "Can I get it in writing? Is there a deadline after which this will expire, like in thirty minutes or something?"

"No, not at all, it's good as gold. Or, OK, good as . . . well, it's good. I promise. I'll send you all the details, and you can review them with your choice of real estate lawyer, which we will be happy to pay for. Just deduct the cost of it from your next mortgage payment. It's the least we can do."

"OK, then I guess I'm in."

"Great! She's in!" Stan exclaimed. I heard a flutter of clapping from Fran in the background. "I'll let our chair know right away. Oh, and I'll call Friedrich in Germany, who's got the derivative bet on you, and tell him that he's losing this one."

Gentrification

....

Were you hoping to raise your two kids and designer dog in a low-priced home in that up-and-coming, artsy, shabby-turned-chic neighborhood a bit outside your usual stomping ground? Never discouraged by the presence of established generations of people of color, Old Americans staked their flags anywhere they desired with a colonialist fervor only rivaled by Columbus and his crew. Their approach didn't require chains, murder, or diseased blankets. Increased property taxes, redlining, and "voluntary" relocation proved to be just as effective.

Nearly overnight, community centers were replaced by dog washing parlors, working moms by wine tasters, artist studios by artisan bread shops. Of course Starbucks appeared on every corner in place of bus stops that were no longer needed because the new white families all had three cars. The practice of white, upwardly mobile liberals pushing working-class people of color out of their neighborhoods spread like a plague, causing a great deal of strife, stress, and tension. White neighbors called the police a record five times a day with reports such as "My neighbor's music is too loud" and "My neighbor has a broken-down car outside his house." This bogged down the cops, who had to forego fighting actual crime so that they could act as translators between white people and people of color.

Gentrification has bitten the bullet in Obamistan. As new Obamistanis, the gentrifiers took a long look at where they were living and started to reminisce about the families of color who had first tilled the gardens that were now sprouting their heirloom tomatoes. They had nightmares about rootless young kids of color, lost and wandering from school to school because after moving three times they couldn't remember where their fifth grade classes were. They looked at their adopted "stray" dogs eating gourmet grub in their stainless steel kitchens and wondered if their old families missed them. Eventually they realized that they were living on stolen property. They packed their belongings, called up the old families, and offered their homes back. The former gentrifiers found themselves happy new homes built where the low-income housing projects had been. Now there's a real exchange of cultural harmony in the neighborhood. The yuppies learned to wash their own dogs, and the old neighbors even developed a taste for chai lattes.

Geography

....

Travel is easier and more dynamic than ever before because fuzzy geography is out in Obamistan. "You are from Peru? I was in Baja last summer." That kind of Old American geo-jumble just makes no sense to world-savvy Obamistanis. Obamistanis know where other countries are now. Yes, this also means that people finally realized that Africa is a continent with over fifty countries, not just one giant desert full of black people.

Getting a Job

....

A Testimonial by Abdul-Bari

The first thing I noticed about Obamistan is that getting a job is so much easier. The 100 percent employment rate is definitely an exciting improvement, and so is getting jobs that I am actually qualified for, instead of having to serve frappuccinos to school kids on their lunch hour while my master's degree rots away on my mother's living-room shelf. My cousin, who is an electrician, has also been able to put his best skills to use. Instead of being a living electrical tape dispenser, he's been asked to rewire complex security systems. His labor union is ten times more diverse now and ten times more powerful. I guess the Obamistani government realized that underutilizing its citizens' skills wasn't doing anything for progress.

So right after the election I decided to test the job-market waters. I tossed my barista apron on the floor, donned my pinstriped suit, and walked in for an interview at an elite firm where before I could barely get them to take my calls. With a name like Abdul-Bari, it was hard to get people to invite you inside their control centers. This time was different. When I got there, the receptionist greeted me with a broad smile and welcomed me into the posh lobby. People passing by looked me in the eye and gave me cheery greetings. No one asked me if I was in the right place or if I was there to fix the copy machine. As I scoped out the security guard to see if I was about to be escorted out, the receptionist chimed, "You must be here for the interview!

We are so happy you came in today. I sure hope they hire you on the spot. You look like a very competent young man." I have to admit I looked at her as if she were a little insane. I'm so used to that sentence sounding shaky and scared and more like "You look like a very clean young man" or "I am sure you can be a very reasonable boy."

The receptionist showed me to a comfortable lounge full of couches, where I read a *Fortune* magazine article on the top ten executives in the country. Six of them were people of color. I dug that! The receptionist took my coat and brought me a cup of coffee. She then sent out one of the firm's junior partners. He spent a few minutes giving me pointers and highlighting the kinds of questions that I would be asked. When I thanked him, he said, "Sure thing! I'd do the same if it were my own brother applying for the job." I felt like I was getting the treatment that so many of my white classmates always talked about. I am definitely into this new Obamistani culture where everyone gets the same advantages.

But here is my favorite part: During the interview, one of the members of the interview team started to write my name down on the top of his notepad. I leaned in and began to spell it for him. He stopped me and said, "Oh, silly, of course I can spell your name! My son-in-law's name is Abdul-Bari." That nearly threw off my whole game. But once the interview was underway, the tips that Chad had given me in the lobby paid off. It sounded like I already had the job, and before the end of the day, I did. By the time I got home, I had a message telling me I was hired. "I know we said we wouldn't be calling for a while," the message said, "but we couldn't stand to see you go. You just seemed to be one of us, you know? It felt like you were already one of the family."

The Great Obamistani Jambalaya: The Melting Pot Gets Real Flavor

....

Led by elementary school teachers across the nation, Old Americans spent centuries cultivating a crock-pot-slow-cooked image of the population happily floating together in a giant multilingual hot-tub party: the melting pot. *School House Rock*, the educational sound bite of a generation, even memorialized it in a song, "The Great American Melting Pot":

> *America was founded by the English,*
> *But also by the Germans, Dutch, and French.*
> *You simply melt right in,*
> *It doesn't matter what your skin.*

Never mind the plethora of races, ethnicities, and nationalities that were left out of these lyrics or the fact that no one really knew what a melting pot was exactly. For years the idea scared many children into thinking that they were going to melt away like the wicked witch in the *Wizard of Oz*. It is no wonder that integration was resisted for so long. By the time Obamistan was founded, it was long past time for the country to cook up a fresh new stew.

In looking for a new culinary metaphor to represent the country, Obamistanis considered several options. Fitness advocates Jillian Michaels and Bob Harper encouraged the abandonment of food metaphors altogether due to Old America's life-threatening obesity rates, but, well, Obamistanis still love food. Some things just are not going to change. Obamistan longed for something that maintained a comforting, warm, mom's-home-cookin' feel that would make Obamistanis want to devour their country in one whole delectable bite, an image replete with all the wonderful flavors that Obamistan embraces, that would warm hearts and stimulate the senses. And now we have it.

Presenting . . . the Great Obamistani Jambalaya!

After much conversation, this is what the Obamistani Messaging Division settled on. Chowder, pho, shorba, gazpacho, minestrone, and the president's own recipe for daal were all up for consideration, but with its rich history entrenched in the very soil of the country, jambalaya won hands down. It's a dead ringer for all the different kinds of people, places, things, and ideas that Obamistan combines to get its rich flavor. Plus, who doesn't like something that goes great with cornbread? Cornbread is universal.

Just like Obamistan, the Great Obamistani Jambalaya combines all of its remarkable ingredients in one humble pot. It combines a healthy range of meats, fish, and poultry. It nourishes with a medley of vegetables. You throw in an assortment of spices and let the flavors in that pot influence each other for a good long while. Then spoon it over a mixture of white and brown rice. Delish! An extremely versatile dish, jambalaya can be modified to fit all dietary and religious requirements, demonstrating Obamistan's inclusive values. Plus, fitting the frugality of its citizens, it can be prepared on a slim budget without sacrificing any oomph. Unlike the elusive melting pot, the contents of which no one ever tasted, every restaurant in the country serves a version of the Great Obamistani Jambalaya. You can get a real live taste of what Obamistan is all about, any day of the week, just about anywhere. Of course nothing beats the annual Presidential Jambalaya Cook-Off! The National Mall in Washington, D.C., lights up with vendors from all over the country offering samples of their own unique spin on the national dish. It is a favorite event for tourists from across the nation and visitors from all over the world. Jambalaya has become an international smash, leading Obamistani cuisine's growing niche in the global dining experience. Now when people ask, "What exactly is Obamistani food?" you can respond with scrumptious confidence, "Jambalaya!"

⊂[**RECIPE**]⊃

A Jambalaya We Can Believe In

Includes carnivorous, vegetarian, pork-free, and vegan options.

NOTE: The recipe encourages inclusion, so if an ingredient doesn't fit with your dietary needs, seek a substitute before eliminating it completely. The more flavors you include in your Jambalaya the better it will taste!

Ingredients, Components, and Constituents

A lubricating base of:
    ¼ cup oil or margarine

A veritable smorgasbord of protein personalities:
    3 to 4 pounds chicken, fish, tofu, or seitan pieces
    8 ounces Polish, Italian, chorizo, chicken, or Tofurky sausage, cut into ½-inch pieces
    8 ounces shrimp or shrimp-substitute, canned, fresh, or frozen

A heaping serving of organic vegetables from your backyard victory garden:
    1 green bell pepper, chopped
    1 small red bell pepper, chopped
    3 stalks of celery, chopped
    1 cup carrots, chopped
    ½ cup onion, chopped
    1 clove garlic, minced

A treasure trove of global spices found in your pantry:
  2 teaspoons kosher sea salt
  1 ½ teaspoons Worcestershire, Yorkshire, or soy sauce
  ¼ teaspoon dried thyme
  1 teaspoon chopped fresh lemon balm
  Dash asafetida (hing)
  Dash berbere
  ¼ teaspoon each black, white, and red pepper
  As much heat as you and your dinner guests can
      stand from your choice of hot pepper: habanero,
      cayenne, Thai, Scotch bonnet—there's a world to
      choose from!

Drenched in the warm love of:
  4 cups tomatoes, canned or fresh, chopped with juice
  ¼ teaspoon Tabasco, chipotle, or sriracha sauce
  3 cups water, tap or filtered (not bottled)

Warm the oil and spices in a generous pot. Brown the pro-
teins. Add the vegetables. Finally, cover the beautiful mixture with the liquids. Stir gently to make sure that nothing
sticks together or to the bottom of the pot. Let
stew for forty to ninety minutes. Have the
dish blessed by the religious leader of your
choosing. Serve piping hot over eight cups
of cooked wild, brown, or white long-
grain rice. Eat in generous mouth-
fuls served from your fork, spoon,
chopsticks, or handful of flatbread.

Greeting Cards

Remember how you used to get so angry trying to buy greeting cards? You used to stomp out of the stores in a huff because every dad on the Father's Day cards was white. Remember when you complained to that gift shop after you tried to get a card for your mother's birthday but all the cards you found read "Happy Birthday, Mammy!" and had fat black ladies in aprons on them? Remember how you refused to go back into that store and how your friends had to listen to a tirade about it each time you passed by?

Well, get excited. Go back to that same gift shop. Isn't your sister's birthday around the corner?

You won't believe your eyes! In addition to racial variety on cards, you will also find an entire row of cards dedicated to actual issues. People can talk about just about anything now. The trend started with an Obamistani need to bring up issues of racism gently with fellow Obamistanis who were having a tough time adjusting to the new culture. "Hey, we miss you" graced the cover of the first awkward attempt. Inside, the card read, "Isn't it better to be loved than to be racist?" This was a rocky start, but it opened a floodgate of creativity once the greeting card industry realized that it was missing out on a giant marketing opportunity. Now, in addition to cards about racism, you can get cards about coming out to your parents ("Mom, Dad, get ready to go shopping!"), announcing unplanned pregnancies ("Crap. *That* wasn't supposed to happen!"), getting a divorce ("I can't believe he's getting half"), consoling friends after break-ups ("I never really liked that asshole anyway"), and of course the always classic "There's only one thing I'd change about you," which offers the reader a little breath mint when he or she opens it. You can even get a card that says, "I really need to talk to you about something" and has a little wheel that you can circle about to get just the right topic for an addiction intervention. Perfect for nearly every family!

Guantánamo Bay

···

You have probably been wondering what a country does with its offshore military detention facility in a post-racism world. It is a dilemma many countries will face as they follow in the footsteps of the Obamistan—electing leaders of color, teaching accurate history, re-envisioning heroes, but never being afraid to punish those who act against freedom.

So what happened with ol' Gitmo? The first thing Obamistan did was to start paying Cuba a decent rent for the land occupied by American military facilities there. The Castro brothers (more keep emerging) of course use the rent money to improve the farming and education of the citizens of Cuba. Basically, it's a win-win situation.

Next, Obamistani officials had to decide just who to put in the darn place. That was not as hard as it might seem. In fact, there were, as you might expect, a few folks who would not let go of the old ways. But they couldn't be allowed to stay in the country. They were enemies of freedom. Nonetheless, everyone seems to have found his or her own niche. Former Supreme Court Justices Thomas and Scalia share a cell (at their request) and pass the time making paper dolls out of copies of the Constitution. Don Imus and Howard Stern host a morning show and take turns hurling insults at each other, and there were so many Fox News people that they gave them their own studio. They produce a cute little show (*Git-News*) every night to keep everyone informed about all the gossip and goings on at the base. Mel Gibson is the resident corner drunk—finally starring in a role he is good at—and Michael Richards still tries his hand at comedy, though even there he seems to bomb. Rosie O'Donnell wanders aimlessly around mumbling to herself and laughing at her own jokes, but that is not so different from before.

It is not a bad facility. People are treated humanely. They get three square meals a day. They are allowed to worship and pray as they choose. There is a nice gym for them to work out in, and you can't beat the weather down there. When they are not in voluntary reeducation sessions or therapy, they socialize or go for walks, and several of the detainees are writing their memoirs.

Halloween

Halloween in Old America always seemed to slide into the pit-falls of racism. Some kid on a college campus would dress up in a white robe and hood, thinking his "Pope" costume was genius, or would paint black makeup on his face as part of his Shaquille O'Neal costume.

Obamistan wanted Halloween to be a healthy experience free from any racist mishaps, while maintaining the pagan-pilfered play. No kid should be deprived of the opportunity to dress up and wander the streets at night begging for food.

In a surprising yet ingenious move, Obamistan turned Hallow-een into the perfect opportunity to educate kids and parents alike about the rich colorful history of the country. Obamistanis take every available opportunity to teach each other about the people of color who have made this land great, and candy is still a favorite learning incentive for Obamistani kids.

Now when kids come to your house to trick-or-treat, they get extra-special treats. Along with something that will rot their teeth, people hand out something that will grow their minds. The Ministry of Education and Culture created a series of Obamistani flash cards that can be downloaded for free from their Web site. Simply print out the flash cards and staple them to the Halloween candy you give out. That's right, at Halloween a child can now get a Butterfinger and a black biologist, M&Ms and a Mexican mathematician, an Almond Joy and an Asian activist. This way, kids (and that always steady stream of immature teenagers) are naturally discouraged from wearing race-mocking costumes because the day has become a celebration of all the intelligent, innovative, and groundbreaking contributions that people of color have made. Kids who grow up with this tradition rarely don blackface at their college frat parties. Little kids love to trade, compare, and exchange their flashcards with each other, and their parents learn a lot too.

Handshakes

• •

Everyone wants a special handshake. Many Old Americans, though envious of the cool hand moves they saw on *20/20* specials about gangs, refrained from creating their own for fear of provoking members of MS-13 lurking in the shadows. Obamistanis could not wait to come up with their own special way of greeting each other. The French have the triple kiss; the Japanese bow; and Obamistanis . . . do you have to guess?

Of course, Obamistanis don't shake hands—they fist bump. How could one forget that tender yet hip moment between the president and first lady? Obamistanis embrace this with a passion fitting the innovative spirit of the country. There are double bumps, upside-down bumps, and butterfly bumps. There are bumps with kisses, hip bumps, shoulder bumps; and out at the club, of course, there's the booty bump. Don't be shy about bumping out your greetings. People might flinch and duck the first few times you fling your fist toward them instead of saying hello, but eventually everyone will get in the groove. So go ahead . . . bump . . . bump . . . bump . . . bump it up!

Health Care

··

Call up any health care provider in Old America and you were likely to hear this: "You are black? Well, then you know that black people are predisposed to heart disease. We consider *black* a pre-existing condition. We cannot insure you." "You are Chinese American? Well, you probably eat those funny herbs, and we simply cannot predict how they will interact with *real* medicine. We cannot insure you." "Where do you live? In the Cabrini-Green projects? Oh lordy. The asbestos and rat guano you breathe alone disqualify you for coverage. Good grief! I don't even know why you bothered calling."

People of color were forced to walk into emergency rooms just to be acknowledged by doctors. When they arrived, they waited for hours upon hours and then were told that whatever was wrong with them was most likely their fault. When, at the dawn of Obamistan, it was revealed that racism was a significant factor in causing and exacerbating the wide range of illnesses plaguing communities of color, the health care world was shocked. In Obamistan no pre-existing conditions are excluded from insurance policies because the health care industry came to recognize that the biggest pre-existing condition was racism itself.

Many people of color have been able to remove medication as a fifth food group in their daily diet. Some white people have needed an extra prescription or two since they started coping with the stress of having to bear an equal burden for their race. Diseases like hypertension, diabetes, and anemia have migrated to white patients. This trend increased the demand for physicians of color who had firsthand life experience with these side effects of stress. This means that the bus drivers, janitors, and call center operators who all had medical certifications in their "home countries" are now happily seeing patients. The eight million black and Latino medical techs who had been aiding doctors for years have finally been let into medical school and will be open for business in no time. Every Obamistani citizen is issued a comprehensive health care policy. Emergency rooms are so empty that even television shows set there are boring.

History

In the beginning, there was white . . . just kidding. Of course, that's what Old Americans used to think. In fact, take a look at the flow chart below; it will give you a good idea of how Old Americans saw their journey to this moment in time.

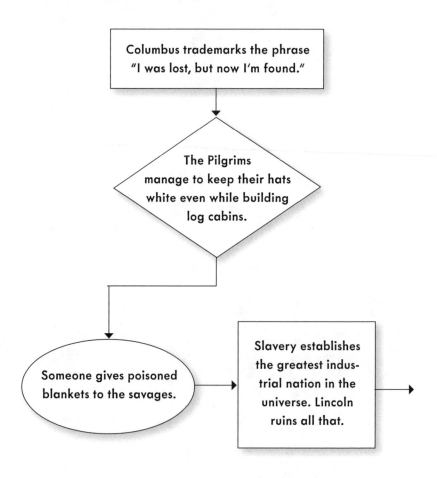

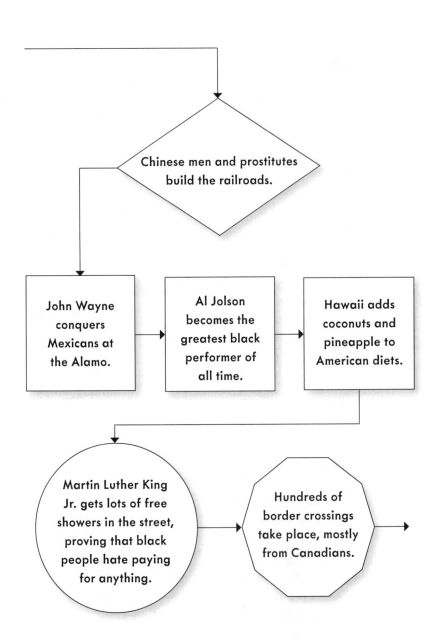

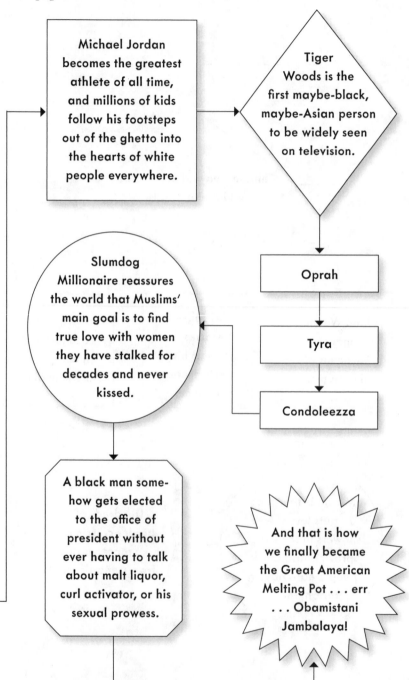

Old Americans were pretty creative in their revisionist traditions. Of course, Obamistanis are passionate about the true history that produced the fall of racism and the country that they hold dear. Take a moment now to create your own trademark Obamistani roadmap to history. Remember to include your favorite milestones and of course mention all the inventors, politicians, Supreme Court justices, activists, and cultural icons of color who helped you be all you are today. Mae Jemison, Victor Ochoa, Sabeer Bhatia, Haunani-Kay Trask, Daniel Hale Williams, Kevin Clash, Dolores Huerta, all your usual favorites. Don't leave it blank! You'd hate for someone to think that you don't know your Obamistani history!

Holidays

....

Obamistan has way more holidays and way more fun!

Instead of everyone in the country being forced to take off Christmas, Easter, and Good Friday, Obamistani workers and students are now allowed to take ten personal cultural holidays per year. These can be applied to whenever their holidays fall without any penalties, pleading, or paperwork. This flexibility is particularly useful for celebrating holidays whose dates change every year because they don't subscribe to the Gregorian calendar. At schools, instead of the absent kid coming back and having to explain where he was the day before, he now hears "Happy holiday!" on his return, because his teachers take fifteen minutes to explain to their classes the special reason that Jacob or Jagdish was out of school for the day. The same happens in the workplace. Offices have taken to the practice with great enthusiasm, except they tend to celebrate the holiday a day early so they can surprise the person with cake (or flan, gulab jamun, or the occasional gefilte fish) at the staff meeting. Happy Diwali everyone!

House Cleaning

....

That woman of color who keeps letting herself into the house next to yours? She is not the cleaning lady. She lives there.

"I Don't Care If You Are Black, White, Green, or Purple . . ."

Power to the purple people! Remember that old refrain? Yep, in Old America, people actually believed that some people were purple, and they embraced them fully! All along, they wondered what they were doing wrong that they never actually met any purple people. But that didn't stop these lovers-of-everyone. They persevered! Folks organized purple-people recruitment events, advertised jobs for purple people, and even set up Internet dating sites that specialized in matching singles with their very own purple mates.

Obamistanis realize that purple people don't exist. Even more exciting, people don't have to make up fictitious races to sound like they are accepting of all.

Immigration

··

A Testimonial by Juan Carlos

I could not believe who showed up at my house yesterday! My aunt and uncle! I was really surprised because they got deported from Old America a few months ago. I didn't think I would ever see them again.

I poured them each a café con leche and waited to hear their harrowing story. I wanted to know how they survived the desert and citizen militias, and what tiny apartment they were living in with dozens of other workers so I could bring them some food. They told me a story so incredible I still can't believe that it is true.

They said that they were sitting at home one day when a knock came at the door. When they answered, it was an immigration officer from the United States. They were scared out of their minds. They had already been deported and could not imagine what more could be done to them to punish them for illegally coming to the United States. They cautiously invited the officer in, fearing that if they turned him away, twenty more would bust in with weapons. The officer sat down and pulled out an envelope. He handed it to them. In it was a letter of appreciation and apology from the U.S. government, thanking them for contributing to the economy and apologizing for terminating their employment prematurely. Also in the envelope were two new U.S. passports, one for each of them.

They were in shock.

When the officer left, my aunt and uncle still did not think they should attempt to cross the border. They knew that there were a lot of angry citizen militia groups stretched across it who would probably think that they had forged their passports and violently force them back into Mexico—or worse. Their curiosity got the best of them, and they cautiously decided to investigate. When they arrived at the United States–Mexico border, traffic was moving smoothly; there was no congestion. This was shocking, as usually there are long lines due to grueling searches of nearly every vehicle that goes across. They pulled up to ask the border attendant what had happened.

"Hi, folks, how can I help you today? Are you headed north?" the oddly cheery officer asked. Shocked, they nodded a silent yes, knowing that saying less is usually safer.

"Great! Let me show you the way." He waved his arm across a horizon of roads like Vanna White unveiling the puzzle on *Wheel of Fortune*. "We've got several new roads, built by the Minutemen, that will make your trip easier. Some of them are even pretty scenic. Would you like a guide for your journey?"

Dumbfounded, they nodded another silent yes. In about thirty seconds, a man wearing a shirt that read MINUTE-MAN: MI TIERRA ES SU TIERRA in giant red-white-and-blue lettering showed up with a big smile, a basket of fruit, and two water bottles filled to the brim.

"You got here fast," my uncle finally spoke.

"That's why they call us Minutemen!" said the cheery white man, pointing to his shirt with pride. "You folks headed up to the states for a good job so you can send some money back home? That is just great. It is so wonderful to see people supporting their strong and growing families. With enough work, hopefully we will get Mexico to a place of prosperity and comfort just like us. So happy to help you get that process started. I'm gonna drive in my jeep just ahead of you, so you two can have some privacy, but if you need anything, just honk. We will be there in no time."

The man gave their car two confident pats on the hood. He walked to his jeep, reached in, and pulled out a magnetic sign that he slapped on the side of his car. It read, "Immigration Escort." He jumped in, looked back at the two of them, and waved to make sure they were ready to go. My aunt and uncle waved back and he started off toward the States.

When they got to Obamistan, they went to see if they could pick up their old below-minimum-wage jobs. The company was thrilled to rehire them, but this time at minimum wage, which they were told was now fifteen dollars an hour. Then the company took them to a hotel for temporary housing, where they could stay for two weeks until they found a good place to live. Not just a place to live—a *good* place to live. Their company makes sure that employees live in comfortable housing so that they are focused and productive at work. After a day at work, the workers at the plant invited my aunt and uncle to join the union, and now with the added pull of all the new immigrants, the union has negotiated for even more improved wages, vacation, and health benefits.

"You want to go eat dinner, mijo?" my aunt asked happily. "Our treat."

"Sure!" I was thrilled! My relatives had never had enough money to take us out before. "What kind of food should we have?" I asked. "We've got the world to choose from, you know."

My uncle chimed in with his usual sense of humor. "I'm in the mood for Obamistani food. Let's get some jambalaya."

Jive Talkin' or Jive Turkey?

Basic small talk was often a train wreck in Old America. Countless awkward conversations started with race-based openers. South Asian Americans would be asked to serve up slushies; black people would be interrogated for their NBA playoff picks. White people were asked, "Are you a Bush or a Baldwin?" Latinos could only accept so many offers to rent their "tropical villas back home."

Try a more personal approach—it's very Obamistani. When you are at a social gathering and see a person you want to start a conversation with, walk up to them and ask them some basic non-race-based questions:

1) "What is your name?" That is always a good place to start. Plus it comes in handy later if you want to talk to the person a second or even third time.

2) "What kinds of things are you interested in?" Avoid any look of surprise when the person answers something outside of a stereotypical career. For example, if you ask an Indian American what he does for a living, do not be surprised at

the answer, "I am a contemporary jazz pianist and composer who just wrote some music for ESPN." This is perfectly normal.

3) If you are still tongue-tied, try using old standards. Talk about the weather, news, and sports. It is also nice to offer a compliment on a person's clothing or the dish they brought to the potluck. You can always talk about the Obamistani service project you did last weekend. Who knew talking to each other could be so easy?

Junk Food

· ·

Much like the liquor stores, convenience stores that sold ice water mixed with neon-blue dye and called it food are no more. In Obamistan, you won't be able to stop off in a neighborhood of color to get twenty kinds of taffy and thirty kinds of dehydrated meat. And you won't find a McDonald's, Burger King, and Wendy's all within a block of the mostly black public school. Those stores have been replaced by organic food markets and natural pharmacies. Now you can get healthful, fair-labor food on the same corner where you used to buy grape soda.

With more people eating healthful food, the price of organic food decreased significantly. Organic grocers, who had been eking out profits by selling exclusively to white people, did some simple math and realized that more customers equals more money. Once they included people of color in their demographic, their profits soared. As organic food businesses thrived, food-related illness plummeted. The lifespans of people of color increased by ten years—which means ten more years of tofu, seitan, and quinoa sales!

Junk food is a dying commodity, so get it while you can. It's not that people don't love Little Debbie anymore; they just realize that Little Debbie created lots of big Debbies with high blood pressure, heart disease, and diabetes. So, if you have a Twinkie in your cabinet, savor it—you might not be able to get one again. But of course, even if you can't, it will last for twenty years, so you can take your time getting around to eating it.

Jury Duty

A Testimonial by Evan

Today I fulfilled my civic responsibility and reported for jury duty! I hated doing that in Old America, but in Obamistan it is lots of fun. The court had a big room for all of us with comfy chairs, wireless Internet, phones, coffee, tea, and pastry. Who could complain? I got more work done sitting there all day than I do at my office.

At the beginning of the day, one of the judges came in and gave us a little pep talk about how serving as jurors is our civic duty as part of a democracy. I vaguely remember this speech from the last time I served, but now, as an Obamistani, there were some things I hadn't heard before.

The judge explained, "Now that racism is over, our system is committed to picking juries that truly represent a cross-section of the country and give a sense of balance and objectivity. We no longer send black defendants to trial with all-white juries. Those juries could barely tell black people apart, let alone decide if a black person was innocent or guilty. Hell, one jury got so confused, they tried to send the prosecuting attorney to jail! Oh, all hell broke loose over the water cooler that day. Anyway, the other judges and I simply got tired of sending innocent people to jail. That's a real drag. Not easy to explain to your kids, let me tell you, especially when the innocent person is their daddy." The judge laughed nervously, squeezed her shoulder with her mic-free hand, and seemed to get lost in her thoughts for a moment.

She shook off her demon and got back on track, "And there will be no more white defendants with all-black . . . Oh, uh, we never really had the opposite problem, so really, what I am saying here is basically, 'no more all-white juries.' And that means no more 'tokened' juries either. You know, the ones that only had one person of color, who would be easily bullied by the other eleven white people? I'm talking actual diversity here, people—you know, like the country we live in? Representative democracy, anyone? Just like the Founding Fathers intended it? Remember? It is not that hard, people." Now she had found her stride. The judge had a bit of failed-comedian-turned-talk-show-host in her.

"Anyway, what this means for you folks is that we will be calling a selection of you forward randomly by name from the list generated by our fancy-schmancy computer system. It doesn't see race. But we have to. So, if we see that the selected group is not racially balanced, we will shuffle some of you in and out until we get a jury that can carry out some well-informed justice. Don't take it personally. It's not personal; it's justice. Do you get what I am saying, people? Can I get a witness? I mean . . . a juror! Ha!"

Laundry

Many Obamistanis were so enthusiastic about living in a truly integrated society that they started washing their colored and white clothes together. This did not turn out very well. You may notice some Obamistanis wearing more pink clothes than they used to. Unfortunately, color and race are not the same thing. Some Obamistanis had to learn this the hard way.

Liquor Stores

••

The next time you want a bottle of Olde English or a Colt 45, look next to the trendy patisserie in the upscale dining district, rather than next to the broke-down auto shop back in the 'hood where you used to go. In Old America, when you wanted a drink, you could find four or five ways to drown your sorrows in the "tougher" areas of town populated by poor people of color. There was a liquor store on every corner, across the street from a bar, across the street from a club, and diagonal from an ATM. Getting drunk was so easy that many of the people who lived in these neighborhoods-turned-liquor-depots simply stayed drunk all the time. This of course made it hard for them to hold down jobs and create stable families, and it made it extra easy to have unwanted pregnancies; but in Old America, that was exactly why the liquor stores were there in the first place.

Don't worry about missing your favorite strawberry blonde Sunday night bartender; she will still be there every week to hear your personal tales of woe. Booze sales are strong in Obamistan. People have a lot to celebrate, and the drink finds its way to every party. There has been a decrease in alcoholism, though. With racial tension lifted, that little nip at the end of the day marks a celebration of a day well lived, instead of a way to shake off the sting or guzzle away the guilt of prejudice and discrimination. Obamistanis may still have sorrows to drown, but none of them come from racism. Now, when Obamistanis drink with racism on their mind, it's to reminisce about the fond farewell they gave all that hatred and tension on November 4, 2008. Crowds of people spanning multiple races cause ruckuses in local bars as they raise their glasses with the toast, "Salud, shalom, and see ya!" Everybody shares a good laugh and knocks back a few cold ones.

Manners

Good manners are a very exciting development in Obamistan. You might find yourself having to do some catching up. Below are a few new etiquette rules that Obamistanis instituted to celebrate the new age.

Instead of speaking loudly when they think someone does not speak English, Obamistanis speak that person's language instead. It is much more effective.

"Brown before clowns!" White Obamistanis get their priorities straight by repeating this fun refrain while they open doors for people of color. In this same spirit, people of color are seated first in restaurants, and no one at the table eats until the oldest person of color takes the first bite.

Double-dip chip dipping. This was a point of controversy in Old America: can you dip a chip into the salsa, bite it, and then dip it in the salsa again? No. Obamistanis are big on metaphor, and self-ishly double-dipping into the pot of wealth that belongs to every-one is an image not lost on Obamistanis. Everyone is due his or her equal amount in Obamistan, so dip once and move on.

Shortening the names of people of color. The next time you meet a man named William, you will realize that his name is not "my boy Billy," "the B-bomb," or "B." In fact, Obamistanis will call him Mr. Patterson. Isn't that nice? If you can't pronounce someone's name, don't give them a nickname or call them by the first letter instead. Obamistanis rock names. Respect!

In Old America it was commonplace to grab, pull, tug, twist, make shadow puppets out of, and wipe your hands on the hair of people of color. You will have to find other ways to occupy your idle little fingers in Obamistan.

There is no more comparing your suntan to the skin of people of color in Obamistan. Your tan is going to fade; theirs is not. This strange phenomenon was never fully explained in Old America, but in Obamistan it is a no-no.

Saying please and thank you is back in style again. White Obamistanis started this tradition off strong the day after the election by sitting down and writing thank-you cards to all their friends of color. Popular sentiments included, "Thanks for being my only friend of color for so long. I hope we can still be close now that I have ten more." "Thanks for never pointing out how much less qualified I am than you, even though I was being paid more." "Thanks for building the railroads." That kind of thing.

Mixed

· ·

"Biracial." "Multiracial." Practice saying these words. They are not hard to say, yet Old Americans persisted in stumbling over, avoiding, and mangling these very simple and clear ways to describe people who, defying all odds, in feats of Frankenstein-like integration, managed to combine more than one race in their singular bodies. For Old Americans one race was hard enough to decipher; throw two or more into the picture, and brains went on overload. The term "mixed" (sometimes pantomimed with a stirring motion) gained popularity as a way to avoid having to spell out actual racial combinations.

Confounded by the intra-body melding of races, Old Americans, as they often did, sought to categorize this phenomenon as either patently good or bad. Thus they often exoticized or patronized biracial and multiracial people, either treating them as precious ("Your parents must have been madly in love to create you!") or accidental ("How in the world did those two races ever find each other?").

When not poking and prodding at the mystery of biracial and multiracial people, Old Americans often assumed that biracial people must be part white. Heaven forbid that two people of color *of different races* get their progeny on! It was common to hear Old Americans describe biracial people as, for example, "half Chinese." Hm. And half what else? White. Yes, that's what they meant. Old Americans treated race like a bowl of vanilla cake batter to which little drops of racial food coloring and dashes of flavor were to be added to come up with any number of shades and tastes. Once again white Old Americans thought of themselves as the original shit.

Unfortunately that cake sank in the oven one too many times. In Obamistan you can just say "biracial" and "multiracial," and it works.

Movies

••

Remember the Old American storylines of nearly every movie ever made: the black guy dies first; the brown guy is a terrorist; and the white guy saves the day? Well, that is over. In Obamistan, when you seek entertainment, you won't be able to predict how the plot turns out.

Obamistan offers a renewed sense of originality. The stale, predictable, "you can tell what is going to happen to him because of his race" color coding of pre-Obamistan movies, TV shows, and popular novels is gone. Now you actually have to pay attention and see what unfolds, which makes moviegoing much more interesting. Hollywood opened its doors beyond its former one-per-race policy so that actors of color were finally able to use their talent in a wide range of parts, even as the competition for those roles increased. A virtual onslaught of talent has resulted, as young people are seeing film and TV as viable career options rather than exercises in remaining strong while doors are slammed in their faces.

White actors are a bit more hard up for roles. But since the roles once reserved for people of color are now up for grabs, white actors' repertoire of skills is growing by leaps and bounds as they get cast to endure gruesome deaths, great defeat, and ego-shattering humiliation. Unfortunately, adaptation is challenging for many of Hollywood's most treasured stars. It became obvious that folks like Tom Cruise were not good actors at all, just very well connected. This cadre of stars has seen the demand for their services plummet. Even with all the method acting workshops in the world, they just can't show any real emotion, but black male actors, with all their life experience, are now hotter than ever, as Hollywood strives to put some real on the reel.

Music on the Dark Side: Rooting It Out

· ·

C-ya, gangsta rap! Wouldn't wanna be ya! For those of you who have been "keeping it real," listening to stories of gun- and drug-running on the streets, you're out of luck. The ghettos disappeared when racism fell. Now there is no need for tall tales and long yarns about "thug life" set to rhyme. Sorry. In Obamistan gangsta rappers are all out of a job. This did cause a slight bump in the unemployment rate of black men, but now that the job-application playing field is leveled, they don't have to resort to life on the street (or pretend life on the street) to make a living. They considered doing "historical rap," but, well, that didn't require as many gold chains.

According to the latest reports, Snoop Dogg has begun using his real name (Cordazar Calvin Broadus) again and has started a foundation with Ice-T to help women get out of prostitution. Suge Knight spontaneously combusted (that happens when the devil reclaims your soul), and 50 Cent is working with the Gray Panthers to organize senior-citizen neighborhood watch groups. Diddy (who was never that convincing of a gangsta) is pretty much the same. He did use his reparations check to finally take some acting lessons. Oh, and of course, Tupac Shakur finally revealed that he has been living large on an isolated private island, which now houses a museum to—who else?—Biggie Smalls.

Music On the Light Side: Out of the Closet

Despite its strong and long tradition, Old American white music often had a hard time finding its voice. White musicians "borrowed" from musicians of color, and when that was exhausted, they started mocking their own whiteness by imitating black and brown music. Songs got so confusing they started to implode.

The lack of racial shame in Obamistan has allowed white people to coin a genre of music similar to R&B (rhythm and blues). R&W (a.k.a. rhyme and whine) used to be called "whiny whiteboy music." But now musicians like Coldplay, Radiohead, and the Killers, instead of taking over the entire rock or alternative categories, can come right out and claim their own racial story: "We are white; we have great lives and lots of luxury, but we just can't help writing songs about how hard our existence is." Let's face it: suffering sells; and it is always nice to listen to people just being themselves.

NASCAR

NASCAR auto racing has been the most widely attended sport in America for decades. Not wanting to lose this status, the sport made some groundbreaking changes immediately after racism fell. Perhaps this indicates that NASCAR had been dying to make these changes but was just waiting for the moment when the fans wouldn't rebel. People of color can now come out of their basements, where they were watching NASCAR at low volumes so that the neighbors wouldn't know they were fans, and actually attend the races without being harassed or fearing for their safety.

A flood of drivers of color are now hitting the tracks. Teams quickly became multiracial. DEI Racing changed its name to Determination, Ecology, and Innovation, to honor the great risk-taking legacy of Dale Earnhardt Sr. In keeping with its family-centered reputation, Hendrick Motors started a foster-care/driver-training program for kids of color. Carl Edwards married a black artist who had been a fan for years; she is now his crew chief.

To top it off, the people at NASCAR got so bit by the wave-of-the-future bug that they decided to go green. The cars all run on biodiesel now, and they've started recycling tires, which had been a big, expensive waste. As a result of this forward thinking, NAS-CAR continues to stay at the top of the list of beloved—and now truly Obamistani—sports.

National Motto: E Pluribus Pluribus!

"In God we trust" is still a fundamental belief in Obamistan, though now Obamistanis openly recognize that "god" takes on as many shapes, colors, sizes, and genders as those who worship.

However, the ancient Latin that represented the country for centuries now seemed in need of a fresh, new sentiment. *E pluribus unum*, meaning "out of many, one," may have been a nice idea, but, sadly, Old America never really emerged as "one" out of the many, did it? Obamistanis are sharp. They believe that forging a nation of connected and concerned citizens requires engagement, learning, commitment, and growth—in other words, a unique gift from each individual. The new Obamistani motto was unveiled promptly after the fall of racism. *E pluribus pluribus* ("out of many, many") reflected an exciting sense of solidarity and a passion for the wide range of people that comprise the country.

The communal spirit of the motto has extended to every corner of Obamistani life. Obamistanis stick up for one another as if they are one giant multiracial family. The next time you see someone cut in line or kids having trouble sharing toys on the playground, just say to the offending party,

"Pluribus, man, pluribus." A friendly smile and a pat on the back usually follow as amends are made. Obamistanis, committed to their international reputation for strength and loyalty, use the motto to put the world on alert: if you mess with one Obamistani, you mess with every Obamistani. They often refer to their fellow citizens as "my posse." Former gang members, replacing the gangs of their streets with the gang of their country, are substituting the motto in place of gang tattoos, and of course Kanye West's new line of Pluribus clothing is quite a phenomenon.

Neighborhoods

If you once lived among tattered houses, dilapidated schools, trash, rodents, and crime-ridden streets; if you woke up every day and had to remind yourself that your home was in the most powerful and developed country in the world rather than an underdeveloped nation in need of humanitarian aid; if you frequently received visits from private-school kids doing community service; if you assumed that police were on your corner to arrest you, not protect you, you may have been living in one of the places Old America called a "ghetto."

In Obamistan your streets are clean, maintained by government workers instead of do-gooding (gawking) volunteers. City-funded trash cans are on every corner. You can drink the water from your faucet, which is clear and fresh instead of foul-smelling and rust-laden. Someone will be by in the next few months to fix your roof and paint your house. The term *projects* has taken on a new meaning as low-income housing is replaced by art centers and community gardens, where local celebrities pop by to help the neighbors cook and make crafts. It's a real Martha-Stewart-meets-Majora-Carter vibe.

Families are now living in beautiful homes with three bedrooms for their kids instead of one. The white people you see in your neighborhood are not there just to scope out cheap foreclosure property but to open day cares where your toddlers can be looked after while you go to work. Your kids will be able to walk to a great school up the street without getting shot at or stopped by the police, and there will actually be books, desks, chalk, pencils, and even teachers! And yes, that's right—that is a police officer cruising past your house. But don't be alarmed. Wave as he beeps his friendly horn. You're in Obamistan now. Smile and say hello to the nice officer!

Pop Quiz: Living

The person who used to live in the house I just bought _____.

a) I have no idea. I am too busy "expecting more and paying less" at Target.

b) relocated to low-income housing. I hear those places are nicer than mine.

c) I'm not sure. I can't see any of the other people in my neighborhood due to the eight-foot fence I just had installed.

d) lives next door in a nicer house. I pop by to bring them their mail and homemade jambalaya.

Answer: d. It's a beautiful day in Obamistan! neighborhoods. Mr. Rogers would be proud.

Oprah

Oprah Winfrey is still queen of the universe, leading the masses toward building positive new lives of self-improvement, personal discovery, global charity, and free cars. Old America did get a few things right.

Oriental

··

The confusion over what to call Asian Americans used to be a real stickler. Surprisingly, some people were still using the word *Oriental* (meaning "from the east"). This usage was rooted in an archaic, flat-earth belief that England was the center of the world and everything else should be seen in geographical relationship to it. Obamistanis now recall that they successfully achieved independence from England, don't live there, and are not the center of the universe from which all points are plotted. This has decidedly improved international relations.

Obamistanis dig the power of a unified Asian American identity, while valuing the multiplicity of experiences within it, and have dropped the ugly habit of using "Chinese" as a catch-all for anyone with nonwhite skin, straight black hair, and a penchant for playing violin. (See "Spanish" for a similar problem.) They have also triumphantly stopped using it to mean backward, stupid, or unintelligible, as in "Chinese fire drill" or "He might as well have been speaking Chinese." In another feat of geography-meets-history, Obamistanis even realize that Vietnam is an actual country, not just a war.

Other Catchy Phrases

A thesaurus is a prudent purchase for your new Obamistani life. Consider getting a pocket-sized one to carry with you. One of the many reasons you'll want to have a compendium of synonyms on hand is that you will have to leave behind racism-based catch-phrases. "You are being a real slave driver" and "She is really cracking the whip," which evoke crippling images of white people lording the leather lash over their stables of enslaved black people, are simply passé. Other phrases like "Let's open the kimono on this a bit" are also unwelcome. Now, if a phrase elicits even the slightest cringe, people eschew it for accurate, clearer non-racist verbiage. This includes all related sound effects and gestures as well, like zinging your hand through the air with a *ckrrrrshhh*.

You may be thinking that this is "political correctness" gone haywire, but even the term *politically correct* was a way to quash basic respectful language. Obamistanis are not fixated on being offended or politically correct—they are stoked on being real. You will find that if you use racism-based language, people will look at you as if they simply don't know what you mean. And they don't. Obamistanis just don't speak that language anymore.

It's not hard. For example, "You're cracking the whip" has now become "You are really encouraging us to work hard." How refreshingly accurate—with absolutely no reference to two hundred years of the brutal enslavement of an entire race! Phrases like "Indian summer" and "ricing your car" have also fallen by the wayside as people realize the error of their prior ways. This also means that catchy suffixes like *Nazi*, *-ista*, and *terrorist* (as in, "You're an eco-Nazi, a fashionista, and a grammar terrorist") have also been removed. Naturally, this has carried over into non-racist, cringe-inducing phrases. People almost never say, "He is pimping you out," or, "She drank the Kool-Aid," and absolutely no one uses "retarded" as a synonym for stupid or incompetent anymore. It has really raised the caliber of conversation out of the gutter.

Paranoia

Paranoia in Obamistan has subsided considerably. As a person of color, you may not be entirely convinced yet that white people are *not* out to get you, but things feel different. They are making eye contact. No, they aren't trying to melt your brain; they are just being polite. You will actually get customer service in stores, and no, they aren't just trying to make sure you are not stealing. And no, people won't ask you to park their cars when you are standing outside that store waiting for your friend to meet you. You will notice that people are opening doors for you instead of closing them abruptly before you get there. That strange clicking noise on your phone is gone, and no, the CIA didn't get quieter bugging equipment. And here is the icing on the cake: you will actually be able to hail a cab. Better yet, that cab is likely to be driven by a white guy. He might even open your door for you, and no, he won't turn out to be an undercover cop.

As a white person, you will also find relief from racial paranoia. You can speak freely about race. No, people of color don't think all of you are racists. You can make friends with them. No, they aren't secretly doing "silly white person" impressions of you for their friends when you aren't around. You can stop wondering if every time a person of color speaks they are playing "the race card." Thankfully, now the race card doesn't even exist. When a person of color reaches into his or her pocket, you can assume he or she is reaching for a business card or cell phone, not a weapon. Walking places will be a lot faster, because you won't be crossing the street to avoid all those scary people of color who hate you for everything your race ever did, said, or thought. You will no longer be seen as "the man"; now you can be just "a man." You will not be held responsible for all the ills of the world, only those that white people actually created. Sure, that is still a lot, but in Obamistan this burden is a little easier to carry.

Police

••

Well, this is the one that you have been waiting for, right? How are the police different in Obamistan? Does Obamistan even need police? Of course. But unlike in Old America, Obamistanis are determined that their police arrest actual criminals, not just people they have decided look like criminals.

This required an extensive reeducation program. After trying a wide range of techniques, including psychotherapy, exposure therapy, gestalt therapy, and even dance therapy, the boys in blue finally responded to one of their own most beloved tools for subduing vicious street mongrels.

The Taser® therapy program has been an enormous success. Cops are shown pictures and asked to ascribe an identity to each image. When they get an answer wrong, they are given fifty-thousand-volt bursts of electronic, nonlethal defensive stun-gun force from a safe fifteen feet away with the highest effectiveness and laser-sight accuracy. The Taser program has proven to be "absolutely the best nonlethal deprogramming tool" and is 100 percent effective against stubborn prejudice. It is the ultimate in reeducation technology.

A recently overheard training session sounded like this:

"Who is this white man in the suit and tie?"

"He looks like my brother-in-law."

"No!" ZAP! "That's Bernie Madoff, the billion-dollar con artist. Who is this white man in the flannel shirt with the gun?"

"He looks like my other brother-in-law."

"No!" ZAP! "That's Albert Fish, the infamous child eater. Who is this brown-skinned man in the white veshti?"

"Uh . . . Osama bin Laden?

"No!" ZAP! "That's the president of this country on a diplomatic trip to Sri Lanka."

It took a lot of work, but you can rest assured that the Obamistani police will do their best to get the bad guys—the real bad guys—and lock them up far away from your home and your loved ones.

Pop Quiz: The Fuzz

A cop pulled me over yesterday because

_____.

a) I am brown-skinned and cops assume that all brown-skinned people are up to no good.

b) I am white and police are stopping white people to prove that they are not racist.

c) I was visiting a friend in a "different" neighborhood. The cop wanted to know if I was lost.

d) Oh, right—my registration is expired.

Answer: d. You might want to brush up on the laws of Obamistan; the police are using them now.

Political Prisoners

....

As expected, Leonard Peltier and Mumia Abu-Jamal were finally released from prison and given full pardons. Their cells are now occupied by Henry Kissinger and Dick Cheney, who, after years of evading capture, were convicted of countless war crimes and crimes against humanity.

Kissinger is handling it fine, becoming a godfather figure to the entire prison system; he has really found his niche. Actually it is pretty much the same niche he filled in the White House. Cheney, on the other hand, is on the brink of suffering a nervous breakdown. He can't take the confinement or the isolation, never mind the waterboarding.

Pollution

....

Did you notice that the sun is shining a little brighter yet you just don't feel like you need that SPF 125 sunscreen you've been carrying around? That's right—ending racism meant the end of global warming. That hole in the ozone layer just closed right up. You see, without racism many corporations had to find ways to scale back, cut down on waste, and dispose of toxins in healthy, clean, and green ways. Before the end of racism, corporations spent tons of money convincing small, underdeveloped countries that their toxic waste was perfect to use as fuel for heating, lubricating engines, and even cooking. When that didn't work, corporate operatives could be caught sneaking powdered toxic waste into the sandboxes of public schools in low-income neighborhoods. With racism gone, corporations found ways to "green up" their toxic acts in a jiffy.

Poverty

Poverty is well on its way to being eradicated in Obamistan. With Obamistanis' newfound enthusiasm for sharing, economic equilibrium is spreading like wildfire. The government—and, truly, the citizens themselves—instituted a zero-tolerance policy toward poverty so that now, unless you have chosen poverty as a spiritual vow, you are simply not allowed to live below a healthy Obamistani standard of living. If you are on the street, hungry, or in need in any way, your fellow Obamistanis will come to your aid without even being asked. No Obamistani wants to see an Obamistani cousin, brother, or parent go hungry, no matter how much they argued at the last family reunion.

Sometimes it gets out of hand. If there is any inkling that you are falling on hard times, Obamistanis will fight over who gets to take you out to dinner, put you up for the night, help with the rent or mortgage, take you grocery shopping, or lend you a suit and drive you to a job interview. Employers, inspired by the values of Obamistani citizens, provide housing accommodations to workers in need. Once workers have a few months of their new living-wage pay saved up, their bosses turn them over to their on-staff real estate agents to get them swiftly and safely into solid homes with all the amenities. Individual wealthy Obamistanis offer their financial advice and networks to help people save, invest wisely, build wealth, and avoid hazardous Ponzi schemes. Overall, the country has prospered in a steady progression based on solid investing practices. Word has it that Obamistan may never see a recession, a depression, or even inflation. Obamistanis even adopted a simple motto to help keep the country on track: "Sharing as she goes, Obamistan grows."

Prisons

··

Prisons, which are always an indicator of the state of any country, are different in a few major ways in Obamistan.

1) The people in prison actually committed crimes. This improvement was a direct result of the police reeducation program, the new racially balanced jury system, and Obamistan's concern with actual justice. Now you don't have to lose sleep over innocent people rotting away in prison and criminals roaming the street, free to harm you.

2) Prisons are much more integrated. With racial profiling removed, the number of people locked up for real crimes began mirroring the population of the country rather than reflecting the prejudices of the system. The prisons look more like the makeup of Congress—a true reflection of the Obamistani people. Prisons have also dismantled their segregation programs, which had been instituted to curtail the interracial gang violence caused by bored correctional officers spreading rumors that someone was going to get shanked over dinner.

3) There are just fewer people there. In fact there are fewer and fewer people in prisons every day. Obamistan provides for its citizens. This means that those who need mental care get it in mental institutions instead of isolation cells. Those who need food, shelter, and money find access instead of stealing them. Employment is at 100 percent, so most petty crimes are unnecessary. Parents raise better kids so that the prison system doesn't see nearly as many twenty-year-olds charged with DUIs, drug crimes, or trafficking in Internet porn. In all, Obamistan is a much safer, more peaceful place.

4) People in prison are paid a living wage for the work they do. This proved to be a remarkable incentive for rehabilitation. Voluntary therapy and educational programs are well attended; inmates emerge as responsible citizens; and recidivism rates have sharply declined. Obamistanis want everyone to be at home and happily enjoying Obamistan, not locked up away from it.

5) Prisoners can vote. Obamistan realized that, in Old America, criminals who hadn't gotten caught had been voting in the country's elections since it was established. In Obamistan, if everyone doesn't vote, no one's vote counts at all.

6) Lastly, the death penalty . . . is dead.

Pronouncing People's Names

···

"I've never heard of anyone with a name like yours!" You won't hear this old crutch anymore. Obamistanis have friends of different races from places spanning the globe. Pronouncing names is no longer a mortal fear. Now, Kazakhstani names are a breeze. Irish, Italian, and English names are suddenly illuminated with meaning; global accents fly out of your mouth as if the floor of the United Nations had been your childhood playground. Nghiem? No problem. Yudhoyono? Rolls off the tongue. Sreenivasan? Piece of cake. Nkosazana? You might even save that one for your firstborn.

If you are still catching up, you might get an odd look or two when you can't immediately pronounce "Chandrasekaran," and you might feel embarrassed. It's OK if you have some work to do. The Internet provides an easy resource for looking up names and pronunciations. You can practice sounding things out in the privacy of your own home.

Luckily, Obamistanis are not afraid to talk to each other, so if you can't figure it out on your own, you can simply ask people. Try this: "I am sorry. I seem to be underexposed to people of your racial group. Though I know there are many ways I can find out more about you without your having to teach me, I've fallen behind on my duties as an Obamistani for the moment. I am so sorry that I have to ask, but could you show me—maybe using pictures or phonics—how to pronounce your name?" Whew. That is a mouthful. Why not just learn how to pronounce things on your own?

Race

Let's cut right to the biggest "people issue" Old America ever had: race, the foundation of America and the foundation of Obamistan. Admit it—you didn't just vote for the best guy, you voted for the black guy. It was fun and exciting and a first for the country. Why not enjoy it? Race is great. It makes life interesting and fun, and it's a blast to find out about the lives of people who seem to be nothing like you. Race is a better playground than Six Flags. If it weren't, people would have gotten rid of it years ago. Unfortunately the soul of the racial Six Flags got sold to the devil, and the playground of race became a den of iniquity. Racism needed to be done away with. That is exactly where Obamistan stepped in. Obamistan smashed racism like the monster truck Bigfoot smashes compact cars. However, Obamistan did not get rid of race. In fact, Obamistanis would argue that trying to get rid of race is actually a racist pursuit.

Obamistan loves its races! This is partly because now everybody gets to have a race. In Old America white people often felt left out of conversations about race because they thought they didn't have a race at all. No wonder they tried to make race itself into a bad thing. One extremist camp tried for decades to proclaim that race was a social construct. These theoretical fanatics now know that race is not a fictional character or an apparition seen only by those who believe in it, like Tinker Bell or the Tooth Fairy. They acknowledge that using race to place one group ahead of others was the real problem. In Obamistan the gift of race is used for good and not for evil.

For you academic types who are wedded to post-structuralist theory, it might be put this way: An original premise was that the essentialist ontological classifications of race would and should recede once America amassed enough cumulative progress to term itself "post-racist." However, as racial scholars have lectured and written for decades, this required reframing. The overarching consensus, bolstered by a preponderance of evidence, is that race per se was never the problem. The impasse was inherent not in the existence of race but in the implementation of racial stratification, racial supremacy, cultural superiority, and de facto caste systems. Is that more clear?

The Race Card

As you enjoy your days in Obamistan, you will want to banish the phrase *the race card* not only from your vocabulary but from your thinking. You may need to work with a sponsor or call the help line to assist you in making this adjustment.

Old Americans got addicted to using the phrase to scare away the topic of race, whack-a-mole style. Thankfully, now the phrase has been cast into oblivion, and people can express themselves freely without fear of being whacked on the head.

This phrase represented Old America at a real racial low point. Sure, segregation and slavery were pretty rough, but the incendiary use of the phrase *playing the race card* was one of the most diabolical inventions of modern Old America. Coined in the midst of the O. J. Simpson trial, the phrase was designed to aid conversations about race but instead led to widespread white paranoia. White people used the phrase like a cudgel, as a way to curtail what they perceived as rampant labeling of even the smallest of their actions as racist. White people hurled the phrase at people of color regardless of the topic. One person of color reported that, when he inquired if he could get chocolate instead of vanilla ice cream for his pie à la mode, the waitress stormed off and complained about her harsh working environment: "I can no longer serve people if the race card is going to be thrown at me like that!" Slowly the race card became a magical tool used to invalidate the voices of people of color in epidemic proportions. It got so out of hand that people of color could barely get through half a sentence before they were interrupted with "You're just playing the race card!" This eventually led to more and more silence from people of color, which may have been the point of the phrase in the first place.

The father of the phrase, legal correspondent Jeffrey Toobin, has since been engaged in a genealogical investigation of his own racial heritage, which has caused him to seek psychological treatment. He realized that he might have a few race cards (mostly spades) of his own on the family tree.

Pop Quiz: Finger-Pointing

History has frequently favored white people; therefore _____.

a) it is in the past, and everyone should get over it.

b) I'm in therapy for that.

c) I flog myself every morning until I bleed.

d) I happily give up my parking space, house, and job to help even the playing field.

Answer: d. E pluribus pluribus!

Reparations

....

A Testimonial by Jamal

I got this check in the mail for—well, I can't even type how much; it is just too overwhelming. It looked like it came from the federal government, because it looked like the tax refund check I got that one time. I hadn't seen a check like that for a while, so I was skeptical. I thought maybe it was an Internet scam. I looked more closely at the check, and it read, "Department of Truth and Reconciliation." Of course I thought to myself, *This cannot be right. When has our country ever been concerned with truth or reconciliation?* So I called the 800 number on the check. Sure enough, someone answers the phone in a cheery singsong voice.

"Hello! Department of Truth and Reconciliation. What can we make right for you today?"

"Um, I got this check in the mail . . . ," I said cautiously.

"That is wonderful! We love hearing from recipients of our programs. Are you First American, African American, or Iraqi?" She asked as if each one of those categories held some kind of prize, like a game show host asking me if I wanted what was behind door number one, two, or three.

"African American," I said, worried that maybe that meant that I had to give the money back.

"Great! I am very sorry for the delay in our country's repaying your ancestors for all the work they did to build up the economic structure of this nation. Without them, we really would never have become the country we are today."

"OK, wait . . . what?"

"Did you have any questions about cashing the check?"

"No, I mean . . . I can cash it?"

"Yes, of course. This one won't bounce. Now, do you have any unpaid student loans?"

"Um, yeah, about sixty-five thousand dollars' worth."

"Wow! School sure has gotten expensive over the last several years, hasn't it? Well, I will send you the forms for you to fill out to have those loans repaid. It is the least we can do for keeping you all out of the good schools for so long. What is your mailing address?"

"Uh . . ." I mumbled my mailing address to the happy lady. I was in a bit of a daze at that point. That was quickly broken by her next question.

"Now, pardon me for being so forward in asking, but do you have any relatives in jail?"

I paused. This was not my favorite question.

"Yeah, my Uncle Charles."

"Did Charles commit a nonviolent crime?"

"Yeah, he was accused of robbing a convenience store, but no one could ever really prove . . ."

"Well, bless his heart," she said, interrupting my knee-jerk justification for the shame of having a family member in jail.

"Well, you let him know that our plan for releasing non-violent offenders, particularly those who committed economics-driven crimes, is well underway. We should have him out in about a month. Get your guest room ready!"

"Wha . . . ?" I was so stunned I could barely eke out more than a grunt.

"Now, one last question, if you don't mind. I don't want to take up too much of your time—Lord knows we've taken enough from you already."

"Yeah?"

"Do you have any children or family members under the age of eighteen?"

"Yes, I do." Again, my worry kicked in, figuring that, like with Social Security, the government was going to foist this burden on the younger generation and my kids would end up paying for the crimes of this country instead of those whose ancestors committed them.

"Great!" She was so enthusiastic about all of this. "You can give me their addresses or have them contact me or visit our office. They will want to fill out paperwork so that they can have their college educations paid for in full. We're sorry to say, though, that we can only cover the first four years; graduate degrees go through a different department."

"Um, o . . . kay. I'll tell them."

"OK, almost done with the interrogation—aw, geez—sorry! I didn't mean to say something offensive. That silly little joke can be a real stinger for our Iraqi callers. Don't worry; I am going to log that in the fine book and pay up for that one. I'm still working on this spontaneous mouth of mine. But anyhoo, where was I? Oh yes, did you want to participate in the Talking Reparations program? If you do, I will pair you up with a white person who will offer you a complete and total, informed apology for the decades of white privilege and racial hierarchy that followed the enslavement of your ancestors. The program is experimental, but so far, with our reeducation program, us white people are doing a pretty good job."

"Uh . . . no, no thanks. Well, could you send me some information about that in case I want to join later?"

"Absolutely. You just take your time; we'll be here! Lastly, let me get your social security number as well. We're going to exempt you from paying the reparations tax. We surely don't want you footing the bill for your own apology!"

Reservations:
The Dinner Kind

....

You will no longer have to "Anglo" your name in order to get a dinner reservation. In Old America it was common for a person of color to have to substitute a white-sounding name for her own so that 1) hosts would actually reserve a table and 2) when she arrived at the restaurant, she could find the reservation instead of a mangled, misspelled version of her name that might take twenty minutes to find on the list, if it were ever found at all. "How exactly is that spelled?" asked Old American hosts as if they were holding their noses just to write down the odd collection of letters that had no business being next to each other, let alone being pronounced all at the same time.

Obamistanis have fully developed race-brains. They love that they live in a multiracial society, and make sure they are informed enough to get the most out of it. They know that their beloved Obamistan means more than that black guy with the "funny name" popping up on the TV screen to give the State of the Union address.

Reservations:
The Land Kind

In creating Old America, colonists forcibly removed an entire race of people to small chunks of crappy land dispersed all over the country and told them to become happy farmers of wheat and pigs. The First Americans (the ones who already lived here, not the Mayflower people) were treated as invaders in their own country. Go, Team USA.

Obamistanis try very hard to give First Americans something that the colonists took away from them at every turn—freedom of choice. Today, former reservations are given the opportunity to claim statehood, become sovereign nation-states, or choose a hybrid of the two. The Obamistani government supports these new nations and states with funding for business and industry. The best farming technology has irrigated the once dry desert landscape to create lush green plains where buffalo are brought back from endangerment. Some of the country's most skilled educators have opened top-notch public schools and universities in First American states, financed by the national pool of tax money that now funds all Obamistani schools equally. Many Obamistanis have given their homes to First American families, who now have the option to leave the former reservations and live three feet from a Starbucks like everyone else. Some First Americans, now among the most economically stable people in Obamistan, keep two homes so they don't have to choose between worlds.

Urban reservations, known as "low-income housing," were abolished altogether. In Obamistan there is equal, adequate housing for all.

School

Were you tired of your kids stealing books from the library, lifting pencils from your office, and trying to sneak their way into the bus that takes the neighbor kids to private school?

Obamistanis realize that it takes a nation to raise a child, not just a village. They want future generations to grow up smart, informed, and well equipped to run the country. To equalize the country's schools, they began with the first priority of any capitalist nation: money. The disparity of funding between the schools in wealthy white neighborhoods and those in poor neighborhoods (usually where people of color lived) had to go. Property tax is now pooled into one federal source and distributed to every school equally.

School buildings were finally improved—no more lead paint, cracked walls, broken desks, missing tools, or televisions in place of working computers. Obamistani children have the best, most updated technology available. How else would the leader of the free world treat its future leaders? Obamistan's public schools, decked out with next-wave computers designed by collaborators from Google, Apple, and Microsoft, run with the connectedness that previously had been reserved for the Old American military planning rooms and the space program.

With learning and teaching conditions improved at public schools, the need for private education disappeared virtually overnight. This was good for even the wealthy, who were increasingly unable to afford to keep their kids out of failing public institutions. Teachers who could not read were finally fired from their jobs teaching reading. Math teachers who had to use calculators to do multiplication tables were removed. History teachers all had to be retrained in the accurate history of the nation, and English teachers finally realized that people besides bald, old white men write books worth reading.

All of this means that Obamistani children are engaged with their learning. They like going to school. In addition, kids of color who are smart and educated are no longer stereotyped as "whitewashed," so everyone comes to school with open minds and finished homework. With the kids more involved in their own educational development, they stopped picking on and bullying each other. The saggy-pants set stopped getting searched for guns, and the trench-coat set stopped carrying them. Security guards all got jobs as art, music, and sports instructors since the newly distributed funding allowed for those programs to be reinstituted; and the metal detectors were all turned into raised vegetable beds for the 4-H club, which has ditched its corporate backing and is funded by selling organic produce to local school districts.

Sharing

···

One of the hardest things for white Old Americans to accept was the idea that they didn't actually earn or deserve all the things they had. Many of them thought that "white privilege" was just like the privilege of getting the car keys from their dads when they were teenagers. Clearly they must have done something right. They didn't realize that it was more like sneaking the car keys out of Dad's safe because your older brother gave you the combination. Or like grabbing the keys to the car that your black friend Marcus saved up five years to buy, piling all your friends into it, and driving it to New Orleans for Mardi Gras. Or like getting a set of gift-wrapped keys to a Porsche on your seventeenth birthday after you totaled the Mercedes you got on your sixteenth. And some white privilege was basically a straight-up carjacking.

In Obamistan, sharing put a swift end to white privilege. To extend the metaphor, Obamistanis save up money to buy their own eco-friendly, fuel-efficient, multipassenger cars with side-impact air bags, and of course, give each other rides to work. Life in Obamistan is like one giant carpool lane. Obamistanis get where they are going together. It is faster; it uses fewer Obamistani resources; and the police leave you alone.

Shopping

A Testimonial by Latisha

Figuring that shopping would be an exciting and very different experience in Obamistan, my sister and I were eager to hit the stores. Once we did, I definitely felt like I had entered a magical place. First, people looked me in the eye instead of up and down. No one asked me what I was doing there. No one followed us around the store. Let me repeat that: no one followed us around in the store (you know, to see if we were going to steal something). One girl brought us tea—tea! The salespeople walked up to my sister and asked her how her day was, not "Eh-hem, can I *help* you?" My sister, who was totally oblivious due to being blinded by sparkly objects, told the lady that she was looking for a cocktail dress for an upcoming gala. The salesperson actually believed her! (I mean, it was true, but still.) Continuing to shock me, the salesperson even paid attention to my sister while she was describing what she was looking for in a dress, instead of looking past her at the white customers, figuring they would spend more money. The salesperson also showed us a few dresses, and when we said we didn't want to pay that much for a dress, she responded, "Yeah, we think it is a bit on the pricy side too." Usually when I say I don't want to pay $1,600 for a dress, I get scoffed at and then shown either to the door or to the clearance rack. Instead she took us to a special room in the back where they keep a stash of the best-quality, best-priced garments for their favorite customers. "This is where we keep the special finds that we don't want just anyone to get."

The room was full of lovely clothes. My sister did all she could to restrain herself as she picked out three items that she was interested in.

"Great! Would you like to try them, or would you like me to have Michelle put them on for you? She is built about the same and has a similar skin color, so you can see how the dress hangs and complements your look without having to bother with getting undressed yourself."

My sister agreed, and we both looked at each other because we'd heard the phrase "similar skin color" before. We had no idea who was going to come out of the dressing room. Sure enough, out came Michelle. She was the same height, weight, and yes, skin color as my sister. As she came out of the dressing room, a few other women came into the back room, whom I gathered were fit models as well. It seemed like they had a stand-in for every type of customer who could arrive. I wondered how this was financially possible, but I suppose in Obamistan, investing in diversity really does pay off.

My sister picked out a darling little sequined red dress for just under eight hundred dollars, half the cost of what we were shown in the first showroom.

"No wonder white people have held onto their money for so many years," my sister said as we left the store with her dress wrapped and boxed and tied with a silver bow. My sister had once bought a Gucci purse but hung it on the door of her condo in case she had to take it back so that she could pay her mortgage. "I won't even have to return this dress next week."

Spanish

....

In Old America, *Spanish* was frequently used as a catchall for anyone overheard speaking Spanish, eating beans and rice, or sporting a Virgin of Guadalupe decal on their car. Old Americans thought that Spanish was a race, not a language or nationality. This reflected a poor handle on basic grammar skills.

Obamistanis get that calling a person "Spanish," unless they are from Spain, is like calling someone "Urdu." You can see how silly that is. People have also stopped asking Peruvians and Ecuadorians, "What kind of Mexican is that?"

In Obamistan, *Spanish* denotes either a language or people from Spain. Though the Spanish language is a common bond for many Latino ethnicities and nationalities, people realize that language alone does not define a race. Obamistanis actively use maps. They know how many countries there are in Latin America—far more than just the ones they used to visit on spring break.

Pop Quiz: Asians

John Cho, George Takei, Ming Na, Ming Tsai, Lucy Liu, Lisa Ling, and Sandra Oh are _____ .

a) the Obamistani Department of Math, Science, and Classical Violin.

b) famous Japanese actors. Which one was in *The Karate Kid*?

c) Communist leaders of China and North Korea.

d) hot celebrities of the same race but different ethnicities and nationalities.

Answer: d. Don't freak out when there's "more than one" in the room. Obamistanis can tell people apart.

Sports

In Obamistan, people can enjoy the friendly competition of sporting events without the bitter sting of racism. There's no more cheering, "Go Cowboys! Kill the Redskins!" *Creepy.* Time to put that thinking away with your old varsity jersey. You might want to check in on your favorite teams: their names and mascots have most likely changed. Now, instead of racist caricatures and big cats, sports teams have taken up the mantles of endangered species specific to their locales, creatures that actually have reason to be angry and fighting for their lives. Besides engaging in good-natured racing, tackling, fighting, and classic American competition, each team donates a portion of its winnings, ticket sales, and fan gear sales to protecting the living thing that it has adopted as its mascot. You might find yourself championing the cause of a few new endangered pals: check out the Juno Polar Bears, Kansas City Sturgeons, Dallas Prairie Chickens, Houston Manatees, Cleveland Dragonflies, and Washington Lobbyists. What fun— and educational for the kids at the same time! You will feel guilt-free as you cheer, "Go, Sequoias! Save the trees!"

Standardized Testing

....

Gone. That was a no-brainer.

Staying Vigilant

···

One important responsibility of every Obamistani is to maintain constant vigilance so that the creepy crud of racism doesn't find its way back into the culture. If you see even the slightest indication that racism is leaking into your country, your Obamistani Spidey sense will ferret it out and sound an alarm, and you will take all necessary action to squash it like a California cockroach.

Here are a few fun, progressively more daring experiments that you can try every so often to see if racism is still really over.

Go to a movie rental store and cruise the DVD section. Check out the covers that have a picture of a white guy with a gun on the front. Is he the hero? Is he an FBI agent or old-school cop, someone you can trust? Now check out the pictures of the black guys with guns. Are they the heroes? Did those stale images of black people as gangsters, cops-turned-bad, or prison escapees creep back into the adventure aisle of the video store?

Get sick. That's right—get really sick. Pick something that requires an emergency room. Now pick a neighborhood. Don't just go to the one where you live—that's too easy. Why not try the one in the former ghetto? See if you can get medical attention within fifteen minutes. Thirty minutes? An hour? Longer? Does the hospital have the medical supplies to help you? If not, you can write the minister of equity for Obamistan; she will make sure your concerns are addressed.

Send your friends of different races to different nightclubs in your neighborhood. Yes, this time stay close to home; it's good to know how things are going down in your own hood. Each of you should have a good time, live it up for a while, dance, have a drink or two. Now, here's the awkward part, especially for you nonviolent types. Pick a fight. That's right, throw a drink in someone's face, hit on that big guy's girlfriend, or heck, slap him on the behind. Start a brawl! See which one of your friends is thrown out of the club by the bouncer and which one receives a "stern talking to" from the manager. Are the cops called? How many curse words are used? Who is referred to with words usually used to describe animals? Are any racial epithets thrown? Who gets handcuffed? Arrested? Did anyone get a good, solid whack on the head with a nightstick? Did the Tasers get fired up? How many?

See how much fun keeping racism in check can be? These little experiments test your fellow Obamistanis, keep them on their toes. Don't be afraid to make sure that they treat everyone equally. When they don't, take action.

Success

∙∙

A wise man once said, "Mediocrity is the biggest boon of white privilege." Sadly, he was right. Now that it is no longer accepted that white people do everything better than people of color, it is much easier for people of color to succeed; but, white people, you will have to get used to having your work scrutinized and evaluated—fairly. This means your half-assed efforts won't be praised as brilliant; they will just be seen as, well, half-assed. So the next time you fall asleep at your desk, your boss won't tell everyone else that you are deep into your creative process. Remember that promotion you thought was in the bag? It might go to the person of color in the cube next to you whose idea you stole last year. You will need to redo your budget since you probably won't be getting that big bonus you are used to. As it turns out, in Obamistan you have to earn the money you are paid.

The first hundred days or so that a white person was in a job, he used to be given a fair chance to make an impact and showcase his skills and vision. Of course for people of color in Old America, job performance criticism set in much earlier. Some were being criticized within a week for not bringing the change they promised, while white people in the same positions would still be finding out where the pens were kept.

The hunt for mistakes by people of color got so bad that people started to report failures that had nothing to do with their jobs. Botched soufflés, using the wrong fork, tripping, offering incorrect greetings, and wearing white before Memorial Day were all given as evidence of people of color's incompetence. At times, white people got so obsessed with criticizing people of color that they forgot to do their own jobs. This brought the country's productivity down significantly.

Obamistanis want to see everyone succeed. Bosses and constituents alike give people of color enough time to do their jobs without breathing down their necks and forecasting imminent failure. This newfound trust in their competency makes everyone more productive, happier, and, of course, wealthier. Though at one point in Old America's history, racism was the fuel that fed capitalism, Obamistan has found that post-racism works just as well, if not better. The Obamistani GDP boasts a 50 percent increase over that of Old America. You will surely enjoy spending those extra post-racism dollars in your wallet!

Tanning and Whitening

Tanning booths and whitening treatments were a bizarre part of life in Old America. It seemed that Old Americans couldn't decide if they wanted to be light or dark, black or white. Some used whitening to become whiter; others used tanning as a way of proving how white they were. It was all a chemical and ultraviolet catastrophe. In Obamistan people "own their tones" and are comfortable in the skins they were born with. Tanning salons and whitening services have shut down. The National Cancer Society is thrilled.

Taxes

An additional "white tax" is charged to people who are descended from or have benefited from the racism that fueled this country for so long. Contrary to what you might think, white people welcome paying the tax. They figure they are getting off easy and recognize that paying a few dollars here and there can't possibly be as painful as laboring for centuries without pay only to be discounted as nonhuman; stricken from voting; held back educationally; forced to live in squalor; assumed to be stupid, lazy, violent, angry, dirty, ignorant, and incompetent; arrested in epidemic proportions; and wrongfully sentenced to death.

Taxi Drivers

∙∙

Are you sick of cabbie communication breakdown? Here is good news. With racism eliminated, many of the doctors, nurses, engineers, and professionals in their "home countries" have been able to maintain their credentials and continue their careers in Obamistan. As a result, taxis are no longer driven only by immigrants who have limited options and long stories to tell about what they used to do. Instead, a wonderful career opportunity has opened for recent college graduates who can use the taxi driving profession to learn the layout of a new town, network, and give their brains a much-needed break from the rigors of academic work. You will be surprised in the next five to ten years how many Wall Street executives will say, "I met my new assistant when he was driving a cab!"

Television

....

Obamistani television is of course more diverse: everyone is represented. Black people are not all child care workers; Jewish people are not all pawn shop operators; Koreans are not all dry cleaners, etc. By now this should be apparent. What is really exciting are the new versions of your favorite TV shows popping up on à la carte cable networks in every region.

Several shows have turned their attention to spreading the Obamistani spirit and to reforming people who have failed to evolve. *Supernanny* now sits white people on the naughty mat when they won't play nicely with others. *Wife Swap* sends Obamistani women to homes all over the world to spread multiracial harmony to deprived cultures, and Monique has teamed up with Sharon Osbourne in a super-sized version of *Charm School* that teaches Obamistani manners to those who simply have not caught up to speed.

And of course, Obamistanis love to dive for their cell phones every Tuesday night to vote for their favorite new pop singing sensations on—what else?—*Obamistani Idols*! Yes, that's right, *Idols*. In the spirit of *E pluribus pluribus*, Obamistan felt it was best to be represented to its pop music fans in a Boyz II Men meets Menudo meets *NSYNC all-Obamistani boy band. They of course have Spice Girl-esque counterparts—the Obamibarbies!—a great hook for Mattel, which now makes dolls that reflect all the girls and boys who want to play with them. In a kind of five-spice-powder approach, there are Salty Barbie, Sweet Barbie, Bitter Barbie, Sour Barbie, and Pungent Barbie. It's a real mouthful of personalities, which has made their celeb-reality show, *Five Flavors of Fun*, a number-one hit.

Terrorism

···

"Terrorists are people who hate your freedom and want to impose their oppressive way of life upon you at home and abroad!" Sound familiar? Old America really had put the spin machine into high gear when it came to independent foreign radicals.

Obamistanis realize that terrorists were just the people that Old America had been screwing over for decades. What a revelation! Hatred doesn't just randomly crop up in brown-skinned people around the world. It is way more likely to grow in the hearts and minds of people who have been crapped on for years. With this newfound clarity, the government found that it was much easier to make amends rather than to wage war on the people it had wronged. This new approach to global relations brought terrorism to an abrupt halt immediately following the fall of racism.

You are wondering if Osama bin Laden was captured. Of course he was. Actually, ol' Osama realized that Obamistani authorities were not going to chop his head off, dunk him in water, make him eat his own feces, or tie him naked to a bunch of men while dogs growled at him. He was happy to come forward. Once he did, he shared his distaste for Old American global imperialism in a calm and rational manner, just as his carefully crafted television persona would dictate. The Obamistani government couldn't agree more. They immediately set forth making amends and helping nations worldwide build peaceful relationships with one another, free from independent and state-sponsored terrorism, settlements, kidnappings, and occupations. The Obamistani government also recalled all the Old American military tanks and weapons that were such a large part of global conflict. Now, not only is there nothing left to fight about, there's nothing left to fight with.

Thanksgiving

A Testimonial by Blue Wing

Let's face it—Thanksgiving blows. The only thing good
about it was getting out of school early when I was a kid,
but that didn't even begin to make up for the torture I
endured. Every year was a repeated charade with half of
the kids in construction-paper Pilgrim hats, eating lunch
across the table from the other half of the kids, stripped
down to their underwear, with painted stripes on their
faces, saying "How!" and extending invitations to their
pretend "first Thanksgiving" feasts. Teachers were no
help, as they were busy cutting out stupid construction
paper feathers and taping them to kids' heads. It got worse
when teachers actually tried to "teach" about the so-called
historic moment. "Oh, Johnny, do you think the Indians
knew how to eat with a fork? No, of course not. They
weren't civilized like us. If you are going to be an Indian
at lunch today, you need to eat with your hands! Right,
Blue Wing?" Riiiiight. Ugh, it's a wonder I learned anything at all in school. Recess brought an onslaught of kids
chasing me around school, chanting, "We smokum peace
pipe?" As I grew older, these same rituals morphed into
adult versions, complete with moccasins appearing on the
feet of coworkers who claimed to be 1/64 Cherokee, who
spent their lunch break cutting out more godforsaken
construction paper feathers for their kids to wear at home.
I have spent my whole life dreading the entire third week
of November. Most people spent the "holiday" gorging

themselves on food, while I spent the day puking out my guts in disgust.

I have to admit that, with the election happening only a few weeks before Thanksgiving, I didn't think that much would change, but my skepticism was replaced by surprise. Talk about a day to be thankful! I was blown away.

"Thanksgiving" has finally ended.

I woke up on the third Thursday of November to find that it was First Americans Day. As I walked out of my house, it felt like the world was entirely made to serve me. My white friends kept calling it "You Were Here First Day" and spent the day giving me gifts, cooking me food, and deferring to my opinion on everything. This did a lot to soften the calluses that had grown on my personality from years of grade school hell. One of my friends started a tradition that is already gaining popularity. She gives homemade quilts to First American families and jokes, "Don't worry—these don't have smallpox."

The day has become a national day of apology, mourning, and education. The Obamistani government announced that First American legislators will get to pass a piece of legislation of their choosing on that day. I can't wait to see what they come up with! I turned on C-SPAN to discover members of the Obamistani Senate reading into the record a list of the many things that have been co-opted from, stolen from, or invented by First American peoples! It shocked me when the scroll at the bottom of the screen stated, "Congress reads First American contributions that made this country great." I especially loved that because I had gotten really sick of people telling me how white men (usually Thomas Jefferson) invented or imported so many of the things that I knew my ancestors had created. No one ever believed me when I explained the brilliance and innovation of the people they thought ran around chopping off heads and dancing with buffalo. It kills me that white people think that alcoholism in First Americans is related to our genetics and not to the way they have treated us.

Back in school, my son's non-First American friends tell me that the nightmare that tormented me—paper hats and feathers and kids making up fake Indian names—has been replaced with a day of meaningful learning for all. They don't mind that non-First American kids have to go to school, since adults get the day off from work and spend the day in school with children doing fun activities. Everyone learns nonviolent communication and conflict-resolution skills. Now when people say "never again," they actually have the tools to back up that statement. I hear that teachers actually know a thing or two about First American history, which still shocks me. My son's friends said that their teachers helped them and their parents build a first-aid kit entirely from plants in the school's garden. Classrooms celebrate everything from the invention of rubber to medicine. Kids learn how to make their own potato chips, rotate tires, and freeze-dry food. Lunch has moved from hell to health as kids learn about the journey of their food from the earth to their plate so they can eat their food with the honor it deserves.

Instead of creating those awful Pilgrim-and-Indian skits that my idiot teachers used to ask me to direct, each non-First American wears the name of one First American child who, had it not been for wars, exterminations, disease, relocation, and the host of tools that were used to systematically remove my people from this land, might have lived a full and prosperous life. My son's friends wrote some pretty touching mini-biographies imagining what each young person's life might have been like had they been given the chance to grow up and thrive. I have to say, at least one of the stories brought a tear to my eye. I never knew that white people could show that kind of compassion. Each of these stories is placed in the Museum of First American History in Washington, D.C., creating an ever-growing sense of all the people and potential that were lost.

While everyone else is at school learning about the real history of the country, First American kids get the day off from school. First American families are able to spend the day together, honoring relatives and making plans for successful futures. My family has decided to move our annual reunion to that day. It's a wonderful, fun time for all of us. For me it sure beats calling in sick to work, hiding out at home, and checking up on my grandmother every year to make sure she hasn't made good on her threat to crash her neighbors' dinners by screaming and waving a tomahawk outside their windows. My grandmother is wily like that, but now she's happy; and I love watching her sit in her favorite rocking chair, telling stories as her great-grandkids play joyfully all around her.

That's So Dark

Now that *black* is used properly to refer to a racial category, it is no longer used as a descriptor for all the worst things in the world. People no longer use the word *dark* to mean "evil," "wicked," "ugly," "dirty," "bad," "looming," "sinister," "psychologically twisted," "disturbing," "Darth Vader-esque," or as a descriptor for all things negative. No more black comedy, black magic, or black spots on your soul. Gone are the "dark sides" and "dark moods." Of course that means that *white* no longer means all things good, as in "white magic," "white lies," and "white supremacy."

Obamistanis have the words to say what they really mean; for example, instead of "dark comedy," people say "twisted comedy," "taboo humor," or "sinister story." Magic is easily described as "harmful" or "harmless." White lies are accurately called "lies." Obamistanis have developed a love affair with honest vocabulary. Thesaurus sales have increased tenfold. Did you know you had so many useful words at your disposal?

Toilet Paper

Have you noticed a strange lack of pudgy, ruddy-cheeked, white baby faces in the toilet paper aisle of the grocery store? You're not imagining things. Obamistan realized that cherubic toddlers have nothing to do with a comfortable and clean bathroom experience. Ad executives started to ask their staffs, "Are any of you wiping yourselves with babies? No! People, you are not. Babies make more poop than they ever clean up. They leak constant streams of drool, spew projectile puke with no warning, and stick their fingers in everything. Babies don't even know how to wipe. What were we thinking?" With no obvious answer to the toilet paper question, companies decided instead to promote softness with clouds, kittens, puppies, bunnies, feathers, pussy willows, and baby ducks, which are actually soft. Since *white* is no longer a synonym for *pure, fresh,* and *sanitary,* non-bleached eco-friendly toilet paper has had a wonderful surge in popularity. One brand chose an adorable brown bunny symbol for its recycled, cruelty-free, super-soft bathroom tissue. The brand's sales are soaring through the roof. Take note of these Obamistani trends for your financial portfolio. Investing in Obamistan has proven to be profitable.

Speaking of baby faces, you will find a lot more racial variation on baby food jars, and you won't just find black baby faces on mashed sweet potatoes and Asian baby faces on pureed snow peas. In Obamistan happy, healthy babies of all races share the labels on all the jars in the

baby food aisle. This might seem insignificant at first, but when your toddler grabs for the mashed brussels sprouts because the baby on the label looks like her, you will be grateful!

Tourism: Obamistanis Visit Abroad

Did you get tired of pretending that you were a Canadian when you traveled abroad? It was hard enough to try to navigate your way through a foreign country, but it took extra effort to maintain a fake accent and backstory so that you could avoid the anti-American sentiment that had spread across the world. Now you can retire that Swiss flag pin that you've had on your suitcase for the last twenty years. There is no need to hide your Obamistani identity—the world is pro-Obamistan now!

You may have to answer questions about your new homeland; people in other countries are very curious about its historic accomplishments. Be prepared to respond to inquiries like these: "Is it true that Obamistan has no racism?" "Where do black people live if they aren't in jail?" "What hobbies do white people have to fill the spare time they used to spend trying to take over the world?" "Can I still get cheap decals at the Mexican auto body shops?" "You mean, you are brown-skinned, and you can go anywhere and do anything you want?" "Wait, you know the difference between a Bangladeshi and a Bhutanese?" "My country isn't nearly as great as yours, but do you think we can do what you have done?"

People in other pre-post-racism countries will envy your racism-free bliss. You will want to be honored for the achievements that your country has made, so pull out your flag pin and wear it with pride! Sure, people might ask you about things from the Old American past—the legacy of damaging a lot of countries around the world did not evaporate into thin air. When someone brings that up, find the nearest café for you both to sit down and then give a good listen. A sympathetic ear can go a long way toward healing relationships with the world—just ask Fidel Castro. After you have listened and comforted—maybe even apologized—you can direct him or her to the international wing of the Department of Truth and Reconciliation. There they can collect their amends and any reparations they might be owed. Your newfound foreign friends can trust the healing process offered by the Obamistani government. Show them how you are truly an example to the world. Share the new motto and embrace them with your broad, loving wings, just like your new mascot, the beloved wandering albatross.

You might get tired of explaining all the wonderful new things about Obamistan, so it might be helpful to have a few extra copies of this book with you as you travel. It is always nice to give your hosts a gift!

Uncles

....

A Testimonial by Kerri

I just want to point out right up front that I am in no way—and have never been—a prejudiced person. Not in any way, shape, or form. I was, however, the only girl among twenty-five boy cousins in a crazy family that was definitely prejudiced. They were total rednecks. See, if I am prejudiced against anyone, it's white people! Anyway, I admit I didn't use to know much about people of color. But that was not my fault. The only way I could have known about people of different races in Old America was when they were imported—I mean, bussed to my school district.

Oh, Old America . . . race was so taboo and exciting. Some days I kind of miss it. I remember there were these three black boys in my school; they were all on the track team—well, they *were* the track team. They were mysterious. I really wanted to know them. Actually, mostly

I really wanted to date this one boy, Rodney. He was strong, and his skin used to shine in the sun as he ran the 100-meter dash. But I was also scared of those guys. They were totally unapproachable. They had a lot of attitude. They were really arrogant. Cocky—yeah, that's the word. They were cocky, really cocky—giant and cocky. Even now I get afraid of the dark if I think about those guys; but I just give myself a nice, reassuring caress of my thigh, and everything feels better then.

Anyway, I always wanted to befriend a person of color because it was so *not* a part of my life at home. I wanted to understand what was so different. I suspected that race was a problem in the country, but I didn't know why. My uncles were the biggest thing that kept me from making friends with people of color. When I was fourteen, my uncles sat me down and told me that if I ever brought a black guy home, they'd kill him. You might think that's a hollow threat, but you don't know my uncles. When they say "kill," they mean "shoot dead and smash until the skull shatters." They've got flattened dear heads to prove it and a rifle collection that would have brought Charlton Heston to his knees. Needless to say, as much as I wanted to know those track guys, I stayed away from black men. I didn't need that kind of blood on my conscience. See what I mean? The people in my family are such racists!

Or rather, they *were* such racists. Obamistan has helped my family see people of color in a whole new light. I am so proud of them. At first it was a bit dicey. Before the election, they loved Obama and even voted for him. But when they talked about how great they thought he was, they'd say, "I can't wait until that n-gger gets universal health care passed, so I can finally get my teeth fixed." *Baby steps*, I always say. But now that Obamistan is in full effect, my uncles are renewed human beings! In fact every week they take my daughter to her playdate with Hakim and Hanif, two black Muslim brothers who go to school with her. How's that for catching two birds with one net—black *and* Muslim! My uncles never threatened to shoot either of them or called either little boy a sand . . . you know what. That would have been horrible. They don't live in the sand at all; they live in a McMansion just like ours, down the road from us and across the street from my daughter's best friend Kia-May who is Hmong. I think that one of my uncles is actually a little sweet on Hanif and Hakim's aunt. I have the funny feeling that he's about to ask me for dating advice! The tables have really turned.

The best part is that now I can stop straightening my daughter's hair and saying, "She tans so easily." Now I can introduce my uncles to my daughter's real father—Rodney.

War

War has pretty much subsided. It became too hard to convince soldiers to kill people whom they actually thought of as human beings. The love spread beyond Obamistani borders. Even countries engaged in civil wars started to see the humanity in the people they called their enemies. With the newfound respect among people of different groups, spontaneous negotiations started to erupt on battlefields.

Here is a typical scene that caused the army, navy, and air force to give up on training men for aggression altogether.

"Shoot the raghead!" yelled the commanding officer, who had called in sick to the reeducation training.

"What head? Oh, *raghead*. With all due respect, sir, we don't see people that way anymore," said the soldier, distractedly setting down his rifle as he calmly walked over and kneeled by the side of his commanding officer. "Sir, those are called turbans. People wear them for cultural and religious traditions. They are also quite effective for keeping your head cool in the hot sun. They are not a reason to shoot anyone. Why

176

don't we see exactly what he wants? Then we'll just tell him what we need and take it from there."

With war eradicated, the government still wanted to create opportunities for young people to serve their country and be given something in return. The new GI Bill (*GI* now stands for "growth and investment") sets its sights on tackling issues like global poverty and environmental crises. It still brings young men and women face to face with the gritty reality of the world but without the loss of limbs and psychological trauma. Instead of ending up on disability and lifelong therapy, these new "soldiers" return home ready to open new businesses addressing the economic and environmental dilemmas they have learned about in the field. The Bill provides them with small grants (not loans) to start up projects that enhance the economy.

Without the hatred that fueled war, all that was left to do was to address the root causes. The marines, recognizing that most wars are fought over control of natural resources and economic power and not wanting to give up their reputation for being "first on the scene," bring the heads of major corporations together at a mediation table. It turns out that the marines are exactly the right people to serve as mediators because they are the only ones who can intimidate the heads of corporations enough to get them to follow the rules. So far the program has had a great deal of success. OPEC has agreed to lift restrictions on oil production and instead ration oil long enough to carry the country through the current gas crisis and into the hands of new technologies. This was decided by a coalition of CEOs from the auto and health care industries, representatives from oil-producing nations, and organic farmers. Of all unlikely players, Donald Rumsfeld emerged as a real bridge builder between the United States and the Middle East and finally came out in the open and married the Arab mistress he had been keeping all these years.

Washington, D.C.

....

"I will now recognize the senator from Washington, D.C." Sound strange? Well, it sure sounds good to the citizens of that city— you know, the tiny square between Maryland and Virginia where the White House is? The city with the majority black population which was nicknamed "the last plantation" and that used to issue license plates that said "Taxation without Representation"? Washington, D.C., is now a state with full participation in government, which means actual voting members of both the House and Senate. Yes, the city that houses the offices of the greatest government in the world has finally been allowed to participate in that very government. To top it off, the government now pays taxes to Washington, D.C., which has made property affordable and allowed the black families who had been driven out during the last several decades to move back in. This, in addition to the education funding pool, means that D.C. public schools have the money they've been needing for decades; they have risen from some of the worst schools in the country to number one! That is how the kids in the nation's capital should have been treated all along, don't you agree?

We Are All the Human Race

··

This desperate cry for unity was one of the most disturbing features of Old America. People ran around declaring their zoological classification with such vehemence, it seemed as if they were afraid that they might be mistaken for emus or goats.

Here is the situation: human beings are a *species*, not a race. Sure, "the human race" is a comforting, touchy-feely catchphrase that appears to unilaterally soothe racial tension. It is understandable why people are attached to it, like a favorite baby blanket; it reassures them that all is right in the world. However, Obamistanis are ready to grow up and leave their baby blankets behind.

Obamistanis love being a part of the human species; they also love all the races that make up the species. (If you are a Star Trek fan, you can skip this section. You already know that humans, Klingons, and Ferengi alike have a range of different races within their species.) In the spirit of clarity and unity that is Obamistan, people are learning to say, "We are all human races," which is a great way to cheer on the differences and commonalities that make the human species so great.

Pop Quiz: Humanity

Humans are _____.

a) one big, happy race. When I am asked what race I am, I say, "Human!"

b) a tribe, like on *Survivor*. I hope we get to play the Martians!

c) a blight on the planet. I would rather be a wombat.

d) Oh! I get it. Humans are a *species* made up of lots of different races.

Answer: d. *Yes. Everything you learned in high school sociology class is finally sinking in.*

Welfare

If you are still poor in America, you won't be for long. In the meantime, you will be able to qualify for welfare—at least until poverty is fully eradicated. You will also notice that a ton of white people are on welfare—more than people of color, actually. That has always been the case, although Old Americans were told very different "facts." One of the biggest perpetuated myths was that people of color were clogging the welfare rolls and preventing white people from getting their fair share of government hand-outs. Not to worry. If you are poor and white, you will have the same access to welfare that you had before. In fact you will have to compete with fewer people for that little piece of socialism. There are far fewer people of color in poverty now, so there is much more taxpayer money to be spread around. That is another exciting way that ending racism benefits white people!

White

••

White readers, try this exercise. Say out loud, "I'm white!" Now say it again ten times fast: *I'm white. I'm white, I'm white, I'm white, I'm white. White, white, white, white, white.* Doesn't it feel good to say that? In Obamistan, you can!

In Old America *white* was treated as a dirty word. People would avoid saying it, come up with outrageous alternative words such as *Caucasian, European American,* even *race traitor,* and when all else failed, whisper it quietly as if it were a form of leprosy. It just all got a little bit strange. White people in Old America spent so much energy avoiding being called white and conjuring new names for themselves that it made them seem narcissistic, which just made them look more racist, which made them want to not be white even more. It was a vicious cycle.

One of the things that made being white so hard in Old America was the heaps of guilt that white people carried for the evils that their relatives had perpetrated upon the world. It is true: white people have done some pretty bad things over the years. It was really hard for white Old Americans to admit that people like Hitler and Jeffrey Dahmer and the Unabomber were white, just like them. No matter how much white parents, teachers, activists, and policy makers praised all the good white people had brought the world, Milosevic, Blagojevich, and all those bad whiteys always seemed to bubble to the surface.

In Obamistan it's perfectly acceptable to be white. Take a minute to remind yourself of all the good things that are white, like clouds, snow, kittens, milk, and George Clooney. See, just like people of color, you can take the good with the bad. No race is perfect, is it?

White as the Default Race

....

Pretend you are an Old American. Imagine that someone says, "I saw a man walking down the street." What race is that man? Do you know? Of course. In Old America, the man was white. Why? Whiteness took on a default status, giving Old Americans the sense that white was a kind of "home base" and anything else was some kind of added feature. Basically, *people* meant "white." Anyone else would require a detailed and clumsy description. You could be sure that if a person (or even an object or animal) was not white, it would be deliberately highlighted or at least awkwardly mentioned. White was the comfort zone; not-white was difference. When whiteness was mentioned, usually by a person of color, he or she would be accused of being a racist. White people knew that not mentioning their race positioned them as normal and made everyone else seem like a freak of nature.

Obamistanis have eliminated the notion of white as the default race. The country is no longer seen as some kind of pristine white canvas that has been muddied up by haphazard strokes of random color. Now they mention any and all races, and they especially love to point out whiteness, since this had been neglected for so long. Since the mention of race no longer spurs arguments, riots, or drinks thrown in your face, you can freely describe people's races without trepidation—white people included. So go ahead and tell the story about your idiot white landlord or the sexy white woman you saw on the plane. Put a little light in your life. Start seeing white.

Post Obamistan

"Once You Go Black, You Never Go Back"

A big concern of Obamistanis is what will happen when their beloved, inspirational President Obama is gone. Can Obamistan survive without a fly black president, his fashionable wife, and two flawless children at the helm? If the second or third black president is a loser, will there ever be a fourth? Will a white person ever be elected again? What about other brown-skinned people? Will they do good jobs as leaders, or do they need to spend more time in poverty, oppression, and frustration before they can have their day in the Oval Office? Can a white candidate campaign against a person of color on the slogan of "change" without being called a racist?

These are big questions that only you Obamistanis can answer. This guide can continue to serve as a touchstone for what

Obamistan is and an inspiration for all it can be. Feel free to add your own chapters as you observe your Obamistan. You might want to keep a simple pro/con list to make sure that things are still going in the right direction. If you start seeing things that make it seem like Obamistan is slipping away, rally your fellow Obamistanis and start knocking on doors. That is how change is made.

Appendix

Do You Miss Old America?

It is a simple fact that some of you will wake up in Obamistan and feel very uncomfortable with your surroundings. There are some outliers who just aren't ready to make the change to America 2.0. You at times may find yourself among them.

You might feel that in Old America, people were less complicated; conversations were easier to start; dating, watching television, and even giving gifts were easier. Your black friend always loved getting a Tupac T-shirt; your Mexican friend could always use a five-pound bag of cornmeal; your white friends all loved Pottery Barn gift certificates. Now you have to spend way more time and effort on . . . everything. It gets even more exhausting when you try to see race, but don't freak out about it! How nuanced can you get? Sometimes Obamistan just seems like a drag.

It is OK for you to feel that way sometimes. Change takes adjustment, and that can take time. Be easy on yourself. You might find it useful to seek the help of a professional. In Obamistan many therapists are trained to handle the culture shock that comes from leaving racism behind. You will eventually catch up to the rest of the people in the country who have embraced this change wholeheartedly and are now living happy, joyful, exciting, engaged, prosperous, and community-loving lives. But until you do, there are a few ways you can still visit the racism-loving Old America.

Old American Underground

This guide does not endorse them, but you can still find some underground groups that are practicing the ways of Old America. Much like the underground sex societies of New York's financial district (except much less exciting), you have to know someone in order to get involved. Rumor has it that secret signals, pass codes, and masks are involved. However, the word on the street is that these groups aren't made of the best and brightest Old Americans; so as long as you whisper something related to Ronald Reagan, you're in.

Old American Underground groups are made up of people who simply could not let go. Some people experience a kind of Old America withdrawal. These people can be detected by their nervous behaviors, twitching eyes, lack of familiarity with racial language, and constant looking over their shoulders. They tend to be quite jumpy around people different from them. If you are in a car with friends and you hear that familiar Old American sound of car doors locking as you drive past a person of color, be wary. One of your friends just went into relapse. Pull over and get help right away.

Old America Reenactment Societies

Old America had a long-standing love affair with reenactment societies. The Civil War, the Salem witch trials, even internment camps were all re-created and relived in fields, abandoned farms, and dungeons across the United States. It seems inexplicable, but Old America was a real hodgepodge of personalities. Never wanting to live without a weekend visit to the past, a few troupes of anachronistic societies have formed to re-create the experiences of Old America. It can be alarming when they do unannounced public displays of their reenactments; for example, you might go onto a college campus and see a bunch of people of all one race sitting in one section of the cafeteria while the other races sit separately at their own race-based tables. Don't be alarmed. Simply walk up to the group and ask if they are doing a reenactment of Old America and if you can join in. They will be happy to have you play along.

Old America Theme Parks

A less dorky way to feed your jones for Old America is through an Old America theme park. The Walt Disney Company was the first out of the box to create such places, since they had so many racist images, films, and products already manufactured and ready for use.

Though the proprietors would deny it, the parks are by definition bastions of white privilege. Thus they have become popular places for low-achieving white people to feel a sense of accomplishment and validation. There is also concern about the impact on Obamistani youth, as the parks employ a great number of kids during summer vacation. Young people fill all kinds of jobs from serving refreshments to dishing out prejudice. Obamistani officials keep a close watch to make sure that each young person knows it's just a job.

Once inside the theme park, you'll find that the rides are all about life in Old America. You can choose the race you want to be. With CGI technology, you can actually experience what it was like to be a race other than your own during the Old America times. Choose to be person of color for the day and have your house burned down, be ignored at a lunch counter, fail a standardized test, be denied a job, get gentrified out of your neighborhood, have your hair pawed by a stranger, be called Chinese or Mexican no matter what your ethnicity, be asked "What are you?" repeatedly, be spoken to slowly at earth-shattering volumes, be followed by the police, or be falsely arrested and even convicted and sentenced to life in jail without parole on the slimmest of evidence. Ride the rides as white for the day and enjoy being served first at restaurants, being selected first for jobs, having excellent grades and test scores without doing any work, getting promotions and bonuses without doing any work, dominating the housing boards, and making more money than you could ever put to good use.

For the most part, the parks are a positive way to maintain a connection with history so as to never repeat it. But in a few instances unnamed Old American politicians and corporate executives have had their daily passes to the parks revoked and have been caught sneaking in or gazing longingly from outside the gates.

Rogue Communities

Finally, you might be asking yourself what happened to the Ku Klux Klan and the white-power skinheads? This issue was resolved nicely on its own right after the fall of racism. It was a well-known fact that many members of these groups were full of hate, but also really lonely. Young people interviewed about their decisions to join white-power groups talked about being "losers" or "outsiders" in their communities and schools. White gangs gave them a sense of belonging and community, even if their missions were pretty foul. They would have been just as happy joining groups for stamp collectors, but then they would still have gotten beat up on a regular basis. The big secret was that many white-power movements simply wanted to build community without getting their asses kicked.

After the fall of racism, the KKK and WP groups saw their other white non-hateful brethren having a good time in the new integrated and happy world. Their loneliness grew deeper. Eventually the walls of hatred cracked, and the tears and hugs started to flow. Many of them readily sought out Obamistani reeducation programs and began their lives with a newfound appreciation for those they once hated.

The KKK members did not hate everything. It is well known that many of them were great cat lovers, some with broods that would rival the neighborhood cat lady (who was much sought after for dates by local Klan members). The newly liberated-from-hate KKK started a social club around this love of cats. At the Kool Kitty Kanteen, cat lovers of all shapes and sizes gather and share a drink, pet pictures, and stories about their favorite fluffy friends.

Obamistanis of course have embraced the old haters with a smooth sense of humor. Don't be surprised to see bumper stickers that read, "My best friend used to be a racist!"

Back to list of items   Listed in category: Clothing, Shoes & Accessories > Outerwear

*** White Power / Ku Klux Klan Robe VINTAGE! ****

Item number: 120326796747

You are signed in

Watch this item in My eBay

=Buy It Now price: US $ 19.99   Buy It Now >

End time: Apr-29-09 06:20:49 PDT (20 days 7 hours)

Shipping: US $5.00 (discount available)
Expedited Flat Rate Shipping Service
Service to United States
(more services)

Ships to: Worldwide

Item location: Crawford, Texas

Quantity: More than 10 available

Buyer: User ID kept private

You can also: Watch this item

Get SMS or IM alerts | Email to a friend

Listing and payment details: Show

Get 10% back on all purchases, up to $25. New eBay MasterCard Accounts only. US Residents Only. See Details | Apply Now

Description (revised)

Item Specifics	Vintage Ku Klux Klan Robe	Main Color: White
Style:	Men's and Women's All sizes Available!!	
Material:	100% Hand-picked Cotton	
Type:	Gently Worn (well loved)	
Condition:	May retain some smokey smell	